RECLAMATIONS

RECLAMATIONS

Essays on Neglected Novels and Endangered Ideas

JULIA PREWITT BROWN

BLOOMSBURY ACADEMIC
NEW YORK • LONDON • OXFORD • NEW DELHI • SYDNEY

BLOOMSBURY ACADEMIC
Bloomsbury Publishing Inc, 1359 Broadway, New York, NY 10018, USA
Bloomsbury Publishing Plc, 50 Bedford Square, London, WC1B 3DP, UK
Bloomsbury Publishing Ireland, 29 Earlsfort Terrace, Dublin 2, D02 AY28, Ireland

BLOOMSBURY, BLOOMSBURY ACADEMIC and the Diana logo are trademarks of Bloomsbury Publishing Plc

First published in the United States of America 2026

Cover design by Eleanor Rose
Cover image: Top view of vintage books © Adél Békefi / Moment / Getty Images

Library of Congress Cataloging-in-Publication Data
Names: Brown, Julia Prewitt, 1948- author
Title: Reclamations : essays on neglected novels and endangered ideas / Julia Prewitt Brown.
Description: New York : Bloomsbury Academic, 2026. | Includes bibliographical references and index. Identifiers: LCCN 2026000751 | ISBN 9798216367222 hardback | ISBN 9798216367239 paperback | ISBN 9798216367253 pdf | ISBN 9798216367246 epub
Subjects: LCSH: Fiction–History and criticism | LCGFT: Literary criticism | Essays Classification: LCC PN3463 .B76 2026 LC record available at https://lccn.loc.gov/2026000751

ISBN: HB: 979-8-216-36722-2
PB: 979-8-216-36723-9
ePDF: 979-8-216-36725-3
eBook: 979-8-216-36724-6

Typeset by Integra Software Services Pvt. Ltd.
Printed and bound in the United States of America

For product safety related questions contact productsafety@bloomsbury.com.

To find out more about our authors and books visit www.bloomsbury.com and sign up for our newsletters.

CONTENTS

ACKNOWLEDGMENTS

Two essays in this collection were originally published in journals and have been lightly revised. "The Taboo on D.H. Lawrence" appeared in *Salmagundi* (Fall 2021–Winter 2022, #212-213, pp. 103–14) and "Philip Roth's *When She Was* Good" appeared in *Philip Roth Studies* (Vol. 19, No. 2, 2023, pp. 74–81) under the title "*When She Was Good* and the Eclipse of the Virtuous Heroine: A Revaluation." I am grateful to the editors for permission to reprint the essays.

I wish to thank Amy Martin of Bloomsbury Press for patiently shepherding the manuscript through many stages and for the tact and astuteness of her suggestions for revision. The anonymous readers at the press also offered indispensable advice.

In the years I was writing these essays I benefited greatly, at different times and in different ways, from the literary judgment of Robert Boyers, Bonnie Costello, Shannon Draucker, Samantha Harvey, Carol McGuirk, Christopher Ricks, Barbara Schapiro, and the late Helen Vendler. Not everyone named would necessarily agree with the ideas in this book, but their responses often pushed my thoughts forward.

Finally, I am extremely grateful to my husband, Howard Eiland, for critiquing numerous drafts of the essays and for helping me to clarify crucial questions regarding the novel genre and its historical implications. I have benefited from his generosity and learning for many years now and thank him for his unfailing intellectual support.

Introduction

The essays collected here were written over a ten-year period and are unified by several themes. The epigraph for Chapter 1, taken from Michel Houellebecq's *Whatever* (1994), introduces one such theme: "The progressive effacement of human relationships is not without certain problems for the novel."[1] A mordant irony here, since the progressive effacement of human relationships is also not without problems for human relationships.

The idea that in modern society connection between humans is fraying and that human personalities are becoming more uniform is not new. Honoré de Balzac, Charles Dickens, and E.M. Forster entertain this notion in different contexts, as do modernist writers like Franz Kafka. These and other novelists in the Anglo-American and European traditions are as conscious as Houellebecq of the challenge that the ostensible impoverishment of human relationships presents to the novel form. For if the richness of human character is diminishing in actuality, what will happen to character in fiction? In his last completed novel, Dickens transforms a character into a piece of dinner-furniture that is "kept over a livery stableyard … when not in use."[2]

We use the word *character* in two senses today: to speak of the mental and moral qualities distinctive of an individual human being, and to refer to a person in a story. The inextricable link between these two meanings is present from the beginnings of literary criticism. In the *Poetics* Aristotle writes: "Character is that which reveals moral purpose, showing what kind of things a human being chooses or avoids."[3] Character determines incident, and incident is a reflection of character.[4] Although Aristotle is rarely cited in commentary on the novel today, he does not need to be. His definition of character is woven into the fabric of literature and literary criticism. When Milan Kundera suggested in *The Art of the Novel* (1986) that character is the enduring basis of the novel form, he was thinking in Aristotelian terms.

In novels, the importance of character is difficult to escape. Even though Houellebecq appears to disclaim character in *Whatever*, albeit satirically, the power of his novels depends on the vividness of his characters. Houellebecq's masterpiece, *The Elementary Particles* (1998), appears to thoroughly endorse (again, satirically) the view that life can be understood in its entirety as a scientifically determined collection of particles.[5] But something mediates against this view: human character, especially a character named Bruno. No one who has read the novel can forget middle-aged Bruno immersed in video games in the hospital room of his dying mother, who had abandoned him as a child.

When college students read fiction in literature courses, it is often the characters that interest them most, and their response to characters is usually telling. In Chapter 1, I describe a lively class in which the students were baffled by the behavior of the main characters in a story by D.H. Lawrence. The question of liking or disliking the characters did not come up; the students were beyond that. They felt that the characters did not make sense—their behavior was not "probable" in Aristotle's sense—and that Lawrence was therefore not a good writer. They simply did not know what to make of characters who appear to be living out their lives on terms very different from their own. In short, literature was doing its work: introducing the students to experiences they never had.

At issue here is an idea of education currently in jeopardy: the classical idea of education as a form of awakening or mental growth that is necessarily challenging and even painful, as with Plato's cave dwellers. In recent decades, literary scholars have sometimes excluded from their anthologies or course syllabi authors who might genuinely challenge students, while including others more in keeping with academic fashion or contemporary taste and therefore less likely to give offense. Lawrence has been a victim of this neglect and so has Thomas Carlyle, subject of Chapter 7. Carlyle's *Sartor Resartus*, perhaps the most profound and certainly the most influential coming-of-age story in nineteenth-century English literature, is about a character who manages to become his own therapist. Today's students might well be able to relate to this character's struggles and might benefit from contemplating them, but *Sartor Resartus* has been eliminated from most literature anthologies.

The following nine essays focus on a highly selective set of novels and ideas that are being generally overlooked because of the challenges they pose to contemporary tastes and values. The chapters vary in content. Some concern widely neglected novels whereas others use both well-known and neglected novels to explore endangered ideas.

In addition to novels in a traditional sense, other types of writing such as memoir and experimental fiction receive attention.

Part 1: Contemporary Taste in Fiction opens with essays on two important writers of the past who are objects of this neglect—Lawrence and Philip Roth. Chapter 3 considers the work of five contemporary novelists—Kamala Shamsie, Celeste Ng, Colm Tóibín, Morgan Talty, and Patricia Lockwood—in order to explore the question of whether the idea of *character* is being replaced by the more limited idea of *agency* in popular fiction today. A decline of interest in creating complex characters is evident in three of these writers, but two of them take up the mantle of the novel form and give us sharply defined, multifacted characters whose decisions illustrate their mental and moral qualities.

The focus of *Part 2: Character in Its Moral Context* is on endangered ideas rather than neglected novels. The opening chapter of this section considers the English novel's distinctive point of view on the question of wealth's impact on human character.[6] The idea that being rich—as distinguished from having enough—may be deleterious does not seem to be getting much traction today, but it was a familiar worry of our ancestors, as the novel tradition demonstrates. The second essay in this section takes up questions of suffering and happiness in relation to the figure of the artist. It considers two artists—Oscar Wilde and the largely unknown Mary Ellen Meredith—whose biographical legacies have been overdetermined by the trials they endured. It also considers the ways in which the romantic myth of the suffering artist has limited our appreciation of Kafka's sense of humor. The endangered idea at issue in this essay concerns the spiritual singularity of the artist, whose experience of life is likely to be as unconventional as the work he or she creates.

The last chapter in Part 2 is about an artist whose sense of humor is far from being unappreciated. To the contrary, the popular view of Anthony Trollope's fiction disregards his profoundly pessimistic vision of the modern, bureaucratic state. Trollope sincerely believed in liberal reform and by temperament he was something of a cheery bird, but his novels reveal the way that modern institutions encourage conformity and operate systematically, if inconspicuously, to marginalize the person of conscience.

The pressure of conformity in an administered society tends to make people undervalue more inward, individual responses to life, such as religious feelings that develop outside the church. *Part 3: Creedless Religion and Unbridled Philosophical Speculation*—the two go hand in hand—discusses three narratives that are being neglected today: Carlyle's philosophical novel, *Sartor Resartus* (1833–4); James Baldwin's late memoir, *The Devil Finds Work* (1976); and Keith Waldrop's autobiographical novel, *Light While There Is Light* (1993). At the end of the nineteenth century, Friedrich Nietzsche and others questioned whether morality would be able to survive without traditional religious faith, which had been in decline for at least a century. An increasingly urgent question for our own time runs in the opposite direction: whether morality can survive *with* religious orthodoxies. Writers who embrace a creedless religion—Carlyle, Emily Brontë, Emily Dickinson, Oscar Wilde, Lawrence, Simone Weil, Baldwin, to name a few—have something important to say to us, but their thoughts on this subject are not always taken seriously because the subject itself is not. The possibility of nondogmatic religion appears to be anathema to many people, as if the only legitimate religious feeling available to human beings is to be found in exclusionary, organized worship, an idea that the writers mentioned above would have greeted with skepticism.

One consequence of conformism, in the present context, is a lack of appreciation of the mission of the novel. "The sole *raison d'être* of a novel," writes Kundera, is to "discover a hitherto unknown segment of existence."[7] The uninhibited prose and unsettling content to be found in the writings of Carlyle, Lawrence, Roth, Baldwin, and Waldrop are being neglected largely because of this spirit of conformity. We may point to other reasons for the neglect, of course, the most relevant being the nature of the publishing industry and the prevailing style of contemporary culture.

In any given epoch, the state of the publishing industry determines how easily good novels are made available to readers, if they are made available at all. The publication history of Waldrop's novel is a case in point.

Light While There Is Light appeared in 1993, decades after major publishing houses had published the works by Roth and Baldwin discussed in Chapters 2 and 8. In the intervening years, American publishing was transformed from a rather small industry, centered mostly on the East Coast, into an industry of multinational conglomerates. Drawing on the research of Dan Sinykin, a 2023 *New Yorker* article tracks the exponential growth of the corporate houses in the 1980s as they swallowed up their competitors, the result being that today's publishing houses operate like hedge funds in which every book acquired "is a bet on profitability." The acquisition process inevitably "functions like an index of risk, creating 'a system in which homogeneity … is encouraged' to minimize bad bets. This system affects all houses, no matter their size." Every season, the five biggest conglomerates "are incentivized to pursue best-sellers, authors whose works can scale into a franchise or movie. Meanwhile, independent publishers and nonprofits such as W.W. Norton and Graywolf Press seek to carve out their own niche in this ecosystem by focusing on books with small but ardent audiences (poetry, the literature of marginalized voices)."[8]

While the limitations of contemporary taste in fiction have led to the neglect of worthwhile novels of both the past and present, the current situation in publishing is thus also a factor. Having abdicated their role as tastemakers, many publishers make selections on the basis of saleability, which is necessarily determined by what sold well yesterday. They may risk publishing the first novel of a young writer whose gifts have been lauded by an older, established writer, but if the novel fails to gain a wide readership, which is usually the case with first novels, the young writer may be "written off as a bad investment." For this reason, most young writers "never receive the attention and care needed for their talent to come to maturity."[9] If they are willing to conform to market preferences, which lean heavily toward homogeneity of subject and style, they may prosper, but if they are driven to do what the novel can do—discover "a hitherto unknown segment of existence"—they may have to seek out one of the small presses that, as a rule, are too financially strapped to effectively promote their work.[10] Occasionally first novels do appear on the lists of the big publishing houses and do well, but the system as a whole works against young talent. And the same constraints apply to old talent, because it's the big publishing conglomerates that now decide which authors of previous generations to bring out in new editions.

When Waldrop wrote *Light While There Is Light*, he had already established himself as a poet; his first collection of poems, *A Windmill Near Calvary*, had been a Finalist for the National Book Award for Poetry. Any editor working in one of the big houses in the 1960s or 1970s would have very likely been ready to consider his first novel. But Waldrop turned to fiction in the 1990s; thus a small, independent press in Los Angeles ended up publishing the novel. It was reissued in 2013 by Dalkey Archive Press, a slightly larger press with offices in Illinois, Dublin, and London. When the founder and publisher of Dalkey Press died in 2020, the press was bought by Deep Vellum, a small publishing house associated with a bookstore located in Dallas, Texas. Evidently, none of the big publishers were interested in acquiring Dalkey Archive Press, despite its distinguished history in publishing avant-garde writing. The future of *Light While There Is Light* now depends on whether Deep Vellum manages to keep it in print.

It's ironic that the subtitle of *Light While There Is Light* is *An American History*. In any case, my discussion of Waldrop's novel comes last because, in many ways, it best expresses this book's intention: to draw attention to novels neglected because they don't satisfy conventional expectations of what a novel should be.

Expectations of what a novel should be today are largely conditioned by popular taste because there is no longer widespread consensus as to what constitutes good fiction. One critic of late capitalism, Anna

Kornbluh, describes the dominant style of contemporary culture as one of "immediacy," in which the values of speed, flow, and direct expression carry the most authority. Much of the first-person autofiction popular today exemplifies such a style, which for all intents and purposes is inimical to the construction of literary character.[11] Will novels continue to be read if character is no longer understood as a set of potentialities that unfold over time, if even writers see character as a mere prop for conveying the sensation of immediacy? We may assume that novels will continue to be read, and they may even teach us something about our world, but they will not teach us about ourselves, insofar as we are individuated. The narrator of Patricia Lockwood's *No One Is Talking about This* says as much when she addresses readers of the future: "You will be so wise! You will understand everything about our time! And you will know nothing about us!"[12] A consideration of style in fiction will further clarify these historical developments and will be taken up when discussing writers whose prose style has figured in their neglect.[13]

When reviewing these subjects with colleagues, I was often asked whether the project of reclamation is a "method." Had I been asked this question fifty years ago, the answer would probably have been yes. When I entered graduate school in the 1970s, the academy was very different from what it is today because there was still a consensus—a general agreement among literary critics and intellectuals, both in and out of the university—as to the overall aims of literary inquiry, despite the controversies that often arose inside the intellectual community. And leading literary critics in that period, like Lionel Trilling, often wrote for general readers and were well received by them.

That state of affairs no longer exists. The academy is now made up of many fiefdoms, each focused on a specific mode of inquiry, each possessing its own esoteric vocabulary: critical theory, feminist criticism, queer theory, cultural studies, ecocriticism, African-American studies, postcolonial studies, media studies, and more. In the 1970s, I would have conceived of the project of reclamation as a method for challenging the consensus—the generally agreed-upon canon of works considered acceptable for study—much in the way that earlier reclamation projects, like the discovery of Southern slave narratives or the recovery of works like Kate Chopin's *The Awakening*, challenged the consensus in earlier decades. Today, certain reclamation projects have found a niche by focusing on the timeless quality of literary classics; others exemplify a "postcritique" or renewed appreciative criticism.[14] I take a different approach. Here, the critique of received ideas is very much alive, not in a particular critical practice, but in the novels themselves.

The answer to the question of whether the following project of reclamation is a method, then, is no. My aim is to offer a diagnosis of a cultural situation—the decline of complex characters in contemporary fiction; the retreat of certain ideas about art and life; the neglect of particular novels worthy of consideration because they challenge contemporary tastes and values—without presuming to provide a cure. Perhaps the cure would be the project of reclamation itself, but that is for the reader to decide.

PART ONE

CONTEMPORARY TASTE IN FICTION

1

The Taboo on D.H. Lawrence

The progressive effacement of human relationships is not without certain problems for the novel.

MICHEL HOUELLEBECQ, *WHATEVER*[1]

In the 1960s and 1970s, when I was a college and graduate student, D. H. Lawrence's novels were frequently taught at universities alongside the work of other well-established modernists, like T.S. Eliot, Ezra Pound, James Joyce, Joseph Conrad, and Virginia Woolf. Today one rarely sees his name on the syllabi of literature departments.[2] Nor is Lawrence being read outside of universities very much these days, if the shelves at the big retail bookstores may be taken as an indicator. (At the Barnes and Noble in my area, I counted fourteen volumes of Conrad on sale, and only two of Lawrence: *Women in Love* and *Lady Chatterley's Lover.*) Readers who attended college in the last thirty years will likely not remember and revisit Lawrence later in life because they never encountered him in the first place.

When literary critics speculate as to why this is the case, they point to Lawrence's well-known prejudices. Racist, anti-Semitic, and misogynist sentiments occasionally make their appearance in the novels, poems, letters, and in anecdotes about his life. But since similar evidence may be found in Eliot, Pound, and, to a lesser degree, other writers who have retained their place on the modernist syllabus, this cannot explain the diminishing importance of Lawrence who, despite the complaints against him, is universally regarded as a writer of undeniable gifts. To make only a few comparisons: Lawrence's racist and anti-Semitic comments are neither as invidious as those of Eliot nor as virulent as those of Pound.[3] His moments of reductive misogyny pale beside the fullness of his portraits of women characters like Elizabeth Bates in "Odour of Chrysanthemums," whose tragic depth, I daresay, exceeds that of almost any female character found in the writings of his contemporaries.

It happens that an excellent book on the subject of Lawrence's declining reputation appeared in 2002: Gary Adelman's *Reclaiming D.H. Lawrence: Contemporary Writers Speak Out*. Adelman consulted over a hundred well-known poets and novelists, many of whom judge Lawrence to be of great importance to their own work.[4] (John Updike wrote that "as a writer, a magical writer in the way that a fierce wind blows through his work and picks up a scene, a face, an exchange, he cannot be erased from the English literature of this century."[5]) The students in Adelman's undergraduate seminar on Lawrence, however, roundly dismiss Lawrence, delivering in their evaluations of the course an annihilating verdict on his gender politics and fascist sympathies. Yet since students are willing to look past the same faults in other modernists, admiring their writing for other qualities, the question remains as to why Lawrence's imaginative power does not generally appear to be reaching today's students.

The last time I taught D.H. Lawrence was in an introductory course in literature at Boston University about a decade ago. The students were in their first or second year of college and, as a way of exposing them to the complexities of fiction, I assigned Lawrence's short story, "The Horse-Dealer's Daughter."

Set in rural England in the early twentieth century, the story tells of a young woman, Mabel Pervin, who lost her mother at the age of fourteen and is now left destitute by the loss of the family's horse farm. She devotes herself to tending her mother's grave, feeling that "the world of death she inherited from her mother" is far more real than the life she is living.[6] One afternoon the local doctor, Jack Fergusson, sees Mabel walking "slowly and deliberately" toward the center of a muddy pond.[7] When she disappears into its depths, he runs after her, drags her out of the muck, and carries her home. He removes her clothing, rubs her dry with a towel, and wraps her naked in blankets. When she awakens, she is in a daze and, realizing her nakedness, asks who undressed her. When he replies, "I did … to bring you round," she gazes at him for a few minutes and asks, "Do you love me, then?"[8] Before the dialogue ends, Mabel and Jack have decided to marry.

Mabel's question always comes as a shock to the reader. She had barely spoken to the doctor before their encounter takes place and, later in the dialogue, she asks the same question again, this time putting it in more declarative form—"You love me?"—laying claim to the doctor as a possible lover.[9] Earlier that day, when visiting her brothers at the farm, Jack had been shaken out of his "superficial ease" by Mabel's brooding presence; now, his confidence in his identity as a "professional" is totally destroyed: "That he should love her? That this was love! That he should be ripped open in this way! Him, a doctor!"[10]

Until I taught the story in this particular class, I always assumed the shock every reader feels at Mabel's question is one of intuitive recognition that intimacy can arise unexpectedly between two people—that is to say, spontaneously. But there was little recognition of this sort among the students in the class. When I read the scene aloud, the students were flummoxed by it, seemingly unable to understand why Mabel would speak in this way to a man she barely knew, a man she had ignored in the earlier scene. One young woman in the class exclaimed, "*None* of the dialogue between them makes sense!"

Here is how the story ends:

> And she broke into bitter, heart-broken sobbing. "You can't want to love me, I'm horrible."
>
> "Don't be silly, don't be silly," he said, trying to comfort her, kissing her, holding her in his arms. "I want you. I want to marry you, we're going to be married, quickly, quickly—tomorrow, if we can."
>
> But she only sobbed terribly, and cried:
>
> "I feel awful. I feel awful. I feel I'm horrible to you."
>
> "No, I want you, I want you," was all he answered, blindly, with that terrible intonation which frightened her almost more than her horror lest he should *not* want her.[11]

The whole drift of the story was foreign to these students. Its desperate, inexplicable emotions and paradoxes of word and action, the horror and fear framing the entry into marriage, evidently made it difficult for them to believe such characters could ever exist. After the class ended the thought occurred to me that what had made me believe in the characters when I first read the story in college over forty years ago—their spontaneity—was a big part of what made the story preposterous to students today. Why, I wondered? Are relations between men and women so instrumentalized by the rituals of social media that a date is now as premeditated as a job interview? Are dating apps and previews of online images draining romantic encounters of their power and immediacy? The idea seemed absurd. Yet the students' distaste for Lawrence's characters was undeniable. These characters were too excitable for them. Their menacing, contradictory emotions were not believable because they seemed to well up from some place deep in their psyche over which they appeared to have no control.

Human spontaneity in Lawrence's work—and indeed in his life as well—is not the simple, cheerful business that popular culture has often made it out to be. Think of those TV commercials in which an office worker suddenly does something unexpected, like dancing down the corridor of his office, to the comical dismay of his fellow workers. In Lawrence, spontaneity is dangerous and sometimes destructive, but it is necessary to being truly alive. The force of spontaneous love prompted Lawrence to run off with a married woman, Frieda Richthofen Weekley, and Frieda would regret leaving her three children for the rest of her life. Throughout their relationship, Lawrence and Frieda suffered continual eruptions of hostility that left them in pieces, but the marriage endured. It's not uncommon to read in Lawrence's biographies sentences like this: "The tension between Frieda and Lawrence abated after she struck him with an earthenware plate … "[12] Lawrence would make creative use of this fight in *Women in Love*, when Hermione strikes Birkin with a paperweight, "almost breaking his neck, and shattering his heart."

Birkin staggers away and Hermione lies down on a couch and falls asleep. When she awakens she remembers what she has done and considers that she "was perfectly right … she had done what must be done." Meanwhile, Birkin leaves the house, wanders into the open country, "aware that he could not regain his consciousness, that he was moving in a sort of darkness." Yet he is "happy in the wet hill-side." He removes his clothes and sits down naked among the primroses, rolling in the "sticky cool young hyacinths" and covering his back with "handfuls of fine wet grass, soft as a breath," until he attains an ecstasy of happiness and thinks to himself: "It was quite right of Hermione to want to kill him. What had he to do with her? Why should he pretend to have anything to do with human beings at all? Here was his world, he wanted nobody and nothing but the lovely, subtle, responsive vegetation, and himself, his own living self."[13] In many scenes in Lawrence's fiction, characters receive the gifts of the natural world with open hands and are replenished in their solitude, an experience that is likely becoming increasingly unfamiliar to students today.

In a thoughtful review of John Worthen's *D. H. Lawrence: The Life of an Outsider* published in *The New Yorker* in 2005, the novelist and critic Benjamin Kunkel makes an important point about the difference between the way Lawrence was received by an earlier generation and the way he is viewed in the present. Whereas today he is judged for violating certain taboos, "for a generation or two it was common for the sense of accusation to run the other way: to feel that Lawrence, by example of his passion and courage, stood in judgment over us."[14]

This latter attitude toward literature was not confined to Lawrence. It characterized the way many earlier literary critics and teachers tended to think of any serious writer. I remember my teacher Lionel Trilling saying one day, in a graduate class at Columbia, something to this effect, "You don't critique the classics. You let them critique you." He was articulating an approach to literature that has long been out of fashion. Of course, benefits have come from this shift in critical perspective. Professors no longer take an overly pious view of the author or the work of art. They do not allow themselves to forget the limitations placed on an artist's vision by his or her historical epoch. They take the politics of a work of art very seriously. This is all to the good. But there is at least one liability to be considered, a loss that would presumably overshadow much of the utility of the new approach: What will happen if students and readers today are no longer encouraged to take a work of literature to heart, to allow it to seriously impact their way of thinking, or to test the limits of their most private feelings and values?

Take the example of Jane Austen, a writer whose popularity with students and readers has risen in the same decades that Lawrence's reputation has declined. Many instructors teaching Austen at universities in recent years are likely to draw attention to the limitations of her vision, to the fact that the destiny of the heroine is always marriage. They may emphasize the way the heroine challenges the status quo and may implicitly criticize Austen for rewarding her character with such an undistinguished fate. They are less likely to focus on the trenchant moral critique at work in Austen—to give one example, the gradual unveiling of the heroine's self-deception in *Pride and Prejudice*. These approaches are, of course, not mutually exclusive, but once a teacher dismisses Austen's marriage plot as "retro," the student is encouraged to feel a certain superiority to Austen, and so to feel comfortably shielded from her corrosive educative irony, which spares no character, male or female, and no institution, including marriage.

Lawrence both disliked and respected Austen. With characteristic lack of inhibition, he said insulting things about her, calling her an "old maid" and a snob, but he included in *Women in Love* one of the most profound statements ever made about the world she imagined for us.[15] Birkin and Ursula (the woman he loves) go to a flea market, where they discover a beautiful wooden chair, hand-carved during Austen's period. They study and admire its beauty, and Birkin says, "When I see that clear, beautiful chair, and I think of England, even Jane Austen's England—it had living thoughts to unfold even then … " When Ursula reacts contemptuously, saying that *she* doesn't think so much of Jane Austen's England, "It was materialistic enough, if you like—," Birkin replies, "It could afford to be materialistic … because it had the power to be something other—which we haven't … "

Birkin functions as Lawrence's mouthpiece in the scene when he expresses his alarm and sadness over the direction in which human energies had begun to flow in the face of the rampant greed of the Industrial Revolution; he complains that there is "no production in us now, only sordid and foul mechanicalness."[16] Instead of remaining finite, as it had been for countless centuries of agrarian society, the desire for wealth became infinite. The champions of capitalism came to the extraordinary conclusion that the pursuit of material interest and love of gain were basically benign and innocent and would lead through "invisible hands" and the free play of market forces to the "greatest good for the greatest number." In the words of Keynes, it was possible for the nastiest of men, moved by the nastiest of motives, to somehow work for the benefit of us all. Such shallow optimism continues unabated, of course, at a time when global capitalism is repeatedly touted as a good, despite its catastrophic impact on the environment and its increasingly anti-democratic social consequences.

Lawrence recognized in Austen's novels a preeminent witness to the beginnings of his culture's shift away from the agrarian worldview. Her overall investigative concern with money as an independent force that was threatening to take complete control of the lives of human beings who still had "the power to be something other" anticipates his own concerns. Many of her characters fail to draw on that power, but the best of them succeed in some measure.

Despite his pessimism about the deleterious effects of Western rationalism, Lawrence's novels affirm the power of human beings to go beyond themselves, to burst out of the sack of social and historical circumstances that encloses their lives. In both his fiction and his dazzling, eccentric literary criticism, he stands in judgment over us for the waste we have permitted—the waste of our own natures and the defilement of the natural world. His work is easily linked to that of the romantics, particularly to Wordsworth, who famously observed that "we lay waste our powers: / Little we see in Nature that is ours … "[17] Of course, as a reader of Nietzsche and one who lived through the first world war, Lawrence views the future through a darker lens than did Wordsworth, and the emotions conveyed in his work are more extreme. Many would rather not contemplate, let alone experience, these extremes, as Lawrence well knew.

The singularly uninhibited quality of Lawrence's voice likewise sounds extreme to us. To today's readers, who are accustomed to writers with more measured tones, this quality may be more off-putting than any other.[18] Were I to quote from his essay, "Cocksure Women and Hensure Men," which takes on what he calls "the vast human farmyard," many of the people reading these pages would toss them aside, convinced that Lawrence is too dated in his views of the relations between men and women, and too cocksure as a critic, to be taken seriously.[19] Readers today, I suspect, have been conditioned by the cagey personal voice of the contemporary memoir or personal essay in which the author habitually casts himself or herself in a flattering light. It's not often that we encounter a personal essay in which the writer goes out on a limb and challenges the presuppositions or pieties of his audience.

Even in the heyday of Lawrence's popularity, some of his formulations about the instinctive relations between men and women made me cringe. But the pleasure I took in the distinctively personal voice of his fiction and criticism was not greatly diminished by the raw expression of his beliefs. Conscious beliefs make up only a fraction of a novelist's greater imagination of life. The question is: What did Lawrence's scrutiny of human life give us? What did he shed light on that may be essential for us to understand? Many would answer that what Lawrence uncovered, as no other novelist had before him, was the decisive force of sexuality in human relations. The controversy surrounding the novels, especially the historic obscenity trial against the publisher of *Lady Chatterley's Lover* in 1960 in which Judge F.V. Bryson declared the book not obscene, has made this way of characterizing Lawrence's work inevitable.

Putting aside the fact that it's not so much sex but human relationships that forms the strongest theme in Lawrence's oeuvre (and putting aside, too, that in Joyce's *Ulysses*, a work that was banned in the United States until 1933 and in the United Kingdom until 1936, there is far more and far more varied sexual content than in any of Lawrence's novel), let's briefly consider the treatment of sex in Lawrence's most controversial novel.

Lady Chatterley's Lover is set in the industrialized Midlands and is about a young woman married to a baronet, Clifford Chatterley, who is lame and impotent because of an injury sustained in the First World War. Connie Chatterley has an affair with Sir Clifford's gamekeeper, Mellors, and eventually leaves her husband to be with him, but the process by which she comes to this momentous decision is long and intricate because Lawrence is not only interested in Connie. He focuses on her entire milieu, which includes the ravaged landscape, polluted air, and workers of Tevershall, the mining village based on Eastwood, which Lawrence had known in childhood.

Although Clifford's disability makes him a rather heavy-handed symbol of the paralysis of the English upper class, Lawrence's portrait of Clifford as a landowner, successful writer, and industrialist is more complex than critics have generally recognized. Nowhere is Clifford more ostensibly kind and gentle than when he proposes to Connie that she get pregnant by another man and have a son, so that his ancestral estate, Wragby, will be passed on to a male heir. He urges her that by these means she will achieve "an integrated life, that makes a long harmonious thing."[20] Demure, passive Connie requires some time to register the depth of the insult. At first she is sympathetic and consents to his request, but not long after this scene, when she is in her room alone, she takes off all of her clothes and looks at herself naked in the mirror, as if to contemplate the guarantor of Wragby's future. Sadly, she observes "what a frail, easily hurt, rather pathetic thing a human body is, naked ... "[21] But after she and Mellors become lovers, and her body, mind, and spirit achieve the harmonious integration that Clifford reserves for property relations, her confidence in herself finally emerges.

Lawrence came under renewed attack in 1970 with Kate Millett's bestselling feminist manifesto, *Sexual Politics*, a portion of which is devoted to taking apart the view of women in novels by Lawrence, Henry Miller, and Norman Mailer. Millett views *Lady Chatterley's Lover* as a "quasi-religious tract, recounting the salvation of one modern woman" through her exposure to "the mystery of the phallus."[22] She points to the love scene in which Mellors displays his erect phallus to Connie in the morning light and Connie praises its "lordliness." But Mellors is as much in thrall to his phallus as Connie, just as both are in thrall to her sexuality. Nature envelops and directs them both. To Lawrence, the mechanization of life by industry had, at every level of society, severed human beings from their natural intuition and even destroyed sensuality, especially the sensuality of working people, who had been "daunted, daunted out of existence."[23] He views Connie and Mellors as the only genuinely sane people in their world; all the others, from the miners to the artists, are caught in the industrial machine and driven by money, whether they are aware of it or not.

In scrutinizing Miller, Mailer, and Lawrence, Millett identifies different strains of sexism, from Miller's puerile cockcrowing to Lawrence's theory of "phallic marriage," foregrounding these strains rather than other more complex, ambiguous, or contradictory energies at work.[24] In the case of Lawrence, she does not fully credit Lawrence's strong identification with his female characters, his revolutionary portrait of their sexuality, or his sense of the importance of the mutual self-realization and subjective interdependence of lovers. But she is right to point to Lawrence's quasi-religious understanding of sexuality, as other critics had before her. He was not conventionally religious; he repudiated the traditions of both Buddha and Jesus because of their teachings that "the only happiness lay in abstracting oneself from life, the daily, yearly seasonal life of birth and death and fruition." What he wanted to see take place was an embodied reawakening to the natural rhythms of daily life, "the ritual of dawn and noon and sunset."[25] To Lawrence, humanity in general no longer possessed a sense of its cosmic significance, of life as it might be lived in consonance with nature, of sex as an energy that is not "personal" but part of the great natural rhythm of the sun in its relation to the earth. "Oh, what a catastrophe for man when he cut himself off from the rhythm of the year, from his unison with the sun and the earth," he laments, "Oh, what a catastrophe, what a maiming of love when it was made a personal, merely personal feeling, taken away from the rising and setting of the sun, and cut off from the magic connection of the solstice and equinox!"[26] In the spontaneity of mutual arousal and orgasm, human beings have the capacity to achieve the "deepest of all communions," if they can give of themselves. But the ego-driven "cult of personality" often intervenes and proves fatal to this mystic marriage.[27]

A far cry from the clinical present, Lawrence's idea of *transcendent* sexual passion—transcending mere sensuality, mere "cold, nervous, 'poetic' personal sex"—spoke to the sixties generation.[28] Today it just seems old-fashioned, something in the way Hollywood romance films do. Yet whereas Lawrence's fiction is in decline, these films remain popular, in part because of the sentimentality that allows audiences to take pleasure in them and to satisfy their need to believe in love, even while dismissing the plots as kitsch. Lawrence's novels are never sentimental; they evoke transcendent passion in the context of a somber, prophetic critique of Western rationalism—of the mechanization or instrumentalization of thinking and feeling, the money values that have invaded every area of life. Given Lawrence's sacralization of bodily existence, which forms the basis of this wide-ranging critique, it's not surprising that something like a taboo encircles his work in so-called "secular" societies, societies like our own, in which a rationalizing view of life reigns supreme. Insofar as human life processes are increasingly understood in terms of the different mechanisms of authority that manage them—the medical, therapeutic, technological, and governmental powers that we allow to penetrate our lives—Lawrence's novels will offend. Nothing challenges contemporary politics, from left to right, more than the idea of the inviolability of human desire, or the suggestion that the human body is something more than a machine to be directed, treated, managed, or fed.

All of the passages from Lawrence's fiction cited here center on a naked body. The experience of nakedness and the sight of the naked body demand a fearful attention in Lawrence because they expose one's inmost, private self. Lawrence probably would have disdained the casual, superficial view of the body encouraged on Instagram today. It's hardly surprising, then, that many students take a rather narrow view of his work.

Nevertheless, however archaic and however questionable in terms of contemporary notions of gender his sense of the sanctity and cosmic significance of the human body may seem, it forms the basis of some of Lawrence's deepest meditations on human relations. In "The Horse-Dealer's Daughter," it is the doctor's spontaneous rescue of Mabel's body from death by drowning—they go into the water separately and come out together, as in a baptism—that transforms him from a professional who looks at the world with self-satisfied objectivity to a man with an awakened spirit and sense of connection to another person. And, despite her self-destructiveness, Mabel is seen as already more advanced than the doctor in a spiritual sense because, in her grief, she is connected to the body—the dead body of her mother—by means of her daily visits to her mother's grave. Because of this mortal knowledge Mabel "would always hold the keys to her own situation" and would prove herself capable of igniting the romance that ultimately gives her a much better life than the one she has.[29] She is after all a horse dealer's daughter, and not the least among the achievements of the story is its evocation of socioeconomic reality.

In "Odour of Chrysanthemums," when Elizabeth Bates's husband dies in a mining accident, she views his naked, dead body and has an epiphany:

> Her soul died in her for fear: she knew she had never seen him, he had never seen her. They had met in the dark and had fought in the dark, not knowing whom they met nor whom they fought. And now she saw and turned silent in seeing. For she had been wrong ....In fear and shame she looked at his naked body ....She had denied him what he was—she saw it now. She had refused him as himself. And this had been her life, and his life. She was grateful to death, which restored the truth.[30]

Perhaps Lawrence's great subject is not so much the importance of sexual passion, but the presence of death in life, what Hoellebecq means by the "effacement" of human relationships: the many ways we eclipse one another daily, denying our nature and that of others.

In a recent conversation with a student about the impact of smart phones on the daily lives of people of this generation, I remarked that many students seemed to be almost physically attached to their phones. When the student confessed his fascination with the idea of an apparatus body, a computer with agency and free will, I was reminded of Lawrence's description of the "advanced young" of his generation to whom the body had become a "tool of the mind."[31] Whereas to me, the possibility of an apparatus body sounded deadly, to the student it represented freedom from death: the body as an eternally updatable unit. Until that day comes, can we really do without what Lawrence is telling us? No one can replace D.H. Lawrence because no other novelist of his generation showed more courage in exploring the threat that the post-industrial environment poses to what is most alive in human beings and in the natural world.

2

Philip Roth's *When She Was Good*

Philip Roth's death in 2018 and the subsequent publication of Blake Bailey's authorized biography would, under normal circumstances, have led to revaluations of his work that might have opened new ways for us to think about his achievement. Instead, most commentaries tended to focus on Roth's personal relations with women and his alleged misogyny. This was largely owing to a sex scandal concerning Bailey, who had been accused of sexually abusing several women after having groomed them years earlier when they were his middle school students. (Citing the allegations against Bailey, the publisher W.W. Norton halted shipping and promoting of the biography, then took it out of print, whereupon Skyhorse Publishing quickly picked it up.) In *The London Review of Books*, James Wolcott was so eager to locate a possible "affinity" between the author and his biographer that he carelessly misrepresented an early review by Roth so as to suggest that Roth was unconcerned about the sexual abuse of a twelve-year-old girl.[1]

The contradictory atmosphere surrounding Philip Roth—alternately affronted, ambivalent, and admiring—brings to mind the response to his early work. When I first read his unsettling novel of 1967, *When She Was Good*, I was not many years past my Missouri girlhood. The novel shocked me, but it also taught me something, as no other novel had, about what it meant to be a Protestant woman raised in the mid-century Midwest. In the same year another disturbing novel about a young woman, Sylvia Plath's *The Bell Jar* (1963), was published for the first time under the author's name. I learned from Plath's novel too—about the inwardly alienating effects of conventional expectations for women in that period—but Roth's novel prompted me to turn a critical eye on myself and to think in broader terms about my origins and moment in history.

Roth's first two novels, *Letting Go* and *When She Was Good*, are most frequently viewed as self-consciously "literary" productions, rooted in the work of Henry James and Flaubert. It's true that for those schooled in nineteenth-century fiction, the narrative structure of *When She Was Good* must seem familiar, but the novel also came as a rude awakening. When the self-righteous heroine dies at the end, after having almost destroyed the lives of those around her, something more than the death of an individual character was in play. An entire tradition seemed to have come to an end, the tradition of the heroine who, however attractive or intelligent she may be, is distinguished above all by her virtuous character. In Anglo-American fiction, such a heroine appears with the rise of the novel form in the eighteenth century. One of its earliest and most glorious manifestations is Samuel Richardson's *Clarissa* (1748), which tells the story of a young woman whose quest for virtue is continually frustrated by her mercenary family and whose life ends tragically.

Roth wrote and extensively revised *When She Was Good* over a period of four years, and he considered it the best of his early works. The novel tells a similar story, but with an emphasis so brutally satiric that one cannot imagine the tradition of the noble heroine soon rising again. Jane Austen, Charles Dickens, George Eliot, and Henry James all feature the morally admirable heroine. There are a few outliers among the female protagonists of these writers—Austen's Emma Woodhouse will be discussed at the end of this essay—but the figure persists throughout the nineteenth century and is recognizable in early twentieth-century novels by Virginia Woolf and E.M. Forster. She is changed in the later writers, however, because morality itself, particularly sexual morality, is now fundamentally in question. Perhaps the ambiguously conceived rape in Thomas Hardy's *Tess of the d'Ubervilles*, published in 1891, marks the shift away from the conventionally virtuous woman as type, and with Sue Bridehead in Hardy's last novel, *Jude the Obscure*, her "virtue" has become a liability, a force destructive both to herself and to men.

I can think of no serious, historically informed, incarnation of this type coming after Roth's novel, and this is not surprising.[2] In some of the novelists mentioned above, the heroine borders on the saintly, and saintliness has never found a comfortable niche in secular literary genres like the novel. Eliot's Dorothea Brooke is likened to Saint Teresa in the famous Prologue of *Middlemarch* (1871), but Eliot's narrator pursues the comparison with gentle irony. Conscious of the tradition he is playing with, Roth has the heroine of *When She Was*

Good, Lucy Nelson, become infatuated as an adolescent with the life of Saint Teresa, but when her illusions are shattered and she succumbs to her personal rage for justice, her attitude to Saint Teresa changes: "And as for Saint Teresa, that little Flower, the truth was, Lucy couldn't stand her suffering little guts […] [S]he hated suffering as much as she hated those who made her suffer, and she always would."[3]

By the end of the novel, Lucy herself has been canonized—as "Saint Ball-Breaker"—by her husband's Uncle Julian, one of the few characters in the novel with the courage to speak the truth to her.[4] In fact, a signature motif of this genre develops around the reluctance of most people in the heroine's life to be direct with her. Such reticence is perhaps necessary to keeping the story of saintly egotism going, but it is also in keeping with the wryly portrayed habitus of these well-behaved Midwesterners. Most people would rather not confront an intelligent person who is absolutely sure she is right, especially if they are less convinced of their own rectitude.

For example, don't readers want someone to confront Dorothea Brooke about the wisdom of marrying Reverend Casaubon? To say to her, "Why do you want to marry a man twice your age who is about as attractive as a bladder for dried peas to rattle in?" (This is how Casaubon is referred to privately by one of the characters.) And why don't Isabel Archer's friends stage an intervention to warn her against marrying the creepy aesthete, Gilbert Osmond, in James's *Portrait of a Lady* (1881)? But the characters surrounding these heroines often tend to idealize them. And why not, when the authors themselves idealize them, despite exposing their illusions? The morally superior heroine's illusions arise from inexperience, or the vanity of inexperience, and are therefore forgivable.

Lucy Nelson's illusions arise from experience, though, not inexperience. She develops an iron will that most of the people living in her small town do not see, in part because of the cuteness of her appearance—a pretty turned-up nose, straight blond hair, and the petite stature that satirically aligns her with earlier put-upon heroines like Dickens's Little Nell and Little Dorrit. Lucy lives with her responsible but ineffective grandparents, a ne'er-do-well alcoholic father given to violence, and a weak-willed mother. As a child she possesses genuine sweetness, charm, and liveliness, but witnessing her father's violence toward her mother traumatizes her and she becomes increasingly callous and, as a character, increasingly "impossible to like," as Bernard Malamud complained in a letter to Roth.[5]

Reviewers of *When She Was Good* voiced a similar objection to the characters, as if satire were out of the question.[6] But Roth intended the characterization of Lucy to be "pitiless," in the tradition of Flaubert, and throughout Roth's career he insisted on the irrelevance of likeability as a criterion for assessing his characters. To a class of undergraduates at Bard College in 1999 he painstakingly explained, "The great thing about literature is, it doesn't matter if you like Emma Bovary or don't like her. Only one thing matters: Is she interesting?" and he urged them to resist "easy moralizing reactions to characters in literature."[7] Although Roth had Flaubert's objectivity in mind when he created Lucy, the universe he places her in is more like that of a Balzac novel, in which the reader is made aware from the outset that none of the characters will ever get what they most desperately want.

Lucy's abortive coming of age begins with her taking an interest in Roman Catholic ritual when she is fifteen, the groundwork for this initiative having already been laid by the self-righteous Protestant sense of duty inherited from her grandfather. Hardworking, reliable Willard Carroll (his first name alludes to the protagonist of Sherwood Anderson's *Winesburg, Ohio*, published in 1919) is someone whose goal in life above all is "to be civilized." The novel opens with a description of Willard: "Not to be rich, not to be famous, not to be mighty, not even to be happy, but to be civilized—that was the dream of his life."[8] It's significant that Roth does not write "not to be good" because if you are civilized, you *will* be good, according to the logic of the middle-class Protestant. Your "civilized" conduct—in effect, your conforming to propriety—is proof of virtue. The meanness of Willard's childhood in the northwoods of Illinois has made him a kindly and stalwart husband and parent, determined to do right by all the members of his family, including his feckless son-in-law. Roth never spells out the theological underpinnings of Willard's reasoning, but they are legible enough. When his baby sister suffers brain damage from scarlet fever, Willard concludes that God is deaf, but the tragedy does not prompt him to rage against God like Job. It makes him all the more conscious that he has been mercifully spared—that is to say, saved—so as to meet the conventional responsibilities of life.

When Lucy, rebounding from the spectacle of her father's violence, falls under the influence of a Roman Catholic priest and considers conversion, she may as well be trying to build a house on a condemned site. It's true that human nature is corrupt, she thinks; people are sometimes evil. But there is no evidence that she herself is corrupt or evil. Lucy is absolutely convinced that she has "nothing to confess, because I am right and they are wrong."[9] *They* need to improve, not Lucy. Hence, when her prayers to Saint Teresa are not answered and these others fail to improve—her father does not reform, her inept mother keeps forgiving him, and her civilized grandfather does nothing but display his condescending good intentions—Lucy rejects religion and enters a permanent state of personal grievance. From this point on, everyone is at fault but Lucy. It is men above all who fall short—her grandfather, father, and then her hapless husband Roy, who is no match for her all-consuming contempt.

A ball-breaker is a woman who robs a man of his confidence, and the epithet is most often used as a sexist caricature. In Roth's novel its use is fitting, because Lucy is not Roy's victim; she manages to make him *her* victim. In the more unequal societies of the nineteenth century, women were rarely in a position to victimize men. Dorothea Brooke may cause her husband Casaubon to lose confidence in himself as a scholar because she is more intelligent and far-seeing than he, and Austen's Elizabeth Bennet may unsettle Darcy's self-assurance when she initially refuses his proposal, but these women are not ball-breakers in a Rothian sense. In order to develop as human beings at all, or to do justice to their own ideals, they must challenge the man's confidence in his superiority. Even Stella's vindictive campaign against men in Dickens's *Great Expectations* (1861) does not go very far; in the end, she marries a brute who beats her. In mid-twentieth-century America, women had legal and social protections earlier societies did not provide, and Lucy takes full advantage of these protections.

In the economically secure Protestant world I knew as a child in Missouri, women were treated with considerable respect; they wielded authority in families that were often extended since more people remained where they grew up than would be the case later in history. Women managed the home, directed the social life of the family, and oversaw matters of personal and social conduct. If they chose to work outside the home and tried to rise in the workplace, they encountered opposition and prejudice, but in the home they often reigned supreme. As a result, the woman most interested in exercising control over other individuals might very well choose to remain at home, where being a mother and wife could gratify the need for power. Young women who left the home for the workplace did so from curiosity about the world, desire for economic independence, or a sense of adventure, more than from an interest in gaining power over other human beings. Unlike her friend Ellie, a secondary character in *When She Was Good* who is willing to get her feet wet, leave the small town, move to Chicago, and begin a career, Lucy has little curiosity or sense of adventure. Her childhood trauma has rendered her entirely defensive. She seeks to dominate others under the guise of dutifully serving them, and she thus embraces the role of model wife. Roth's plot revises the Longfellow nursery rhyme alluded to in the title, because it's not when Lucy is "bad" that she is "horrid."[10] It's when she is "good" that she wreaks havoc.

When She Was Good is the work of an artist with a passionate interest in understanding the way a particular American woman thinks in her time and place. It includes a variety of female characters of different ages who, like the enterprising Ellie, are drawn in realistic, not idealizing, detail. Whether Roth was a misogynist in his personal relations appears to be a subject of almost obsessive interest. Bailey's 800-page biography does not gloss over or attempt to excuse Roth's more questionable behavior toward either women or men. When Roth didn't get the praise he wanted from reviewers or the unconditional loyalty he demanded of friends and lovers, he could be imperious and vindictive. But there is no indication he reserved this behavior for women. Lustful and always in search of distractions from his unrelenting writing schedule and his marriages, Roth had countless affairs over the years, including affairs with his students before the norms in the academy changed and administrators no longer turned a blind eye to such relationships. Yet it is striking to note how many lasting friendships Roth had with women, and how generous he was in offering them intellectual and financial support. In reading the biography, I was most often reminded of Dickens, who, like Roth, was as passionate in what he gave to others as in what he took from them, and who did not spare himself in his own fiction.

The most damning evidence against Roth comes from Claire Bloom's unflattering portrait in *Leaving a Doll's House: A Memoir*, first published in 1996 but repeatedly invoked in the discussions of Bailey's biography. The image of the "doll house" alludes to Henrik Ibsen's *A Doll's House*, first performed on stage in Copenhagen in 1879. The play explores the suffocating existence of Nora Helmer, a Norwegian housewife who eventually leaves her overbearing husband. Bloom's title suggests that she identified with Nora in seeking to free herself from the oppressive mental world of her marriage with Roth, but the analogy is surely questionable. The life of a provincial housewife in 1870s Norway, with all its legal and social constraints, would seem to bear little resemblance to that of an internationally known actress living a century-and-a-half later in New York and London. Bloom herself performed the role of Nora in a 1973 film of Ibsen's play; it appears mainly to have prepared her to see herself as a victim in a society where it was no longer necessary to do so if she chose not to. In stark contrast is Lucy's conscious refusal to identify with Saint Teresa, to suffer as the saint had suffered and become a contemporary martyr.

Roth came into his own as a writer with *Portnoy's Complaint*, published two years after *When She Was Good*; it was as if exorcising the demonically virtuous shiksa Lucy Nelson was necessary before he could speak in his own voice. But what is at stake in *When She Was Good* is not just Roth's brilliant realization of a particular character. It's his grasp of the entire middle-class American Protestant value system, with its devotion to surfaces—in particular, to veneers of civility and respectability—and its imperial conviction of its own righteousness. The articulate, pathologically self-controlled Lucy masterfully exploits these surfaces as she sails forward convinced of her moral superiority, but in her attempt to bring down her family and the husband whom she has come to despise, she destroys herself. Although the story is set in the 1940s and 1950s, Roth composed it in the 1960s, when America began to implode under the pressure of opposition to the war in Vietnam, the growth of the Civil Rights movement, and the rise of feminism. *When She Was Good* suggests that the plot against America had already begun.

The plot against the virtuous heroine also had already begun—as much as a century and a half earlier with Jane Austen's *Emma*. Lucy's bad-behaving forerunners include, among others, Emma Woodhouse, William Makepeace Thackeray's Becky Sharp, and Flaubert's Emma Bovary, but Austen's creation is notable among them for representing what Harold Bloom saw as a specifically Protestant willfulness. "The heroine of the Protestant will from Richardson's Clarissa Harlowe to Virginia Woolf's Clarissa Dalloway," writes Bloom, is "fated to suffer" and nowhere is her humiliation more brilliantly conveyed than in *Emma*, when the heroine escapes into the shrubbery after "the collapse of visions that have been exposed as delusions."[11] If *Emma* is a "comedy of the will" because it ends in the heroine's moral enlightenment and happy marriage, we might call *When She Was Good* a travesty of the will.[12] In the last chapter Lucy dies of exposure in the snow with her father's love letter to her mother frozen to her cheek. The realization of love, not as an abstract ideal but a living reality, accompanies the sad epiphanies of many of the heroines I have alluded to here. In Roth's bitterly satiric novel, love's reality takes the form of a letter the heroine can't get rid of, and she dies in masochistic enjoyment of complete isolation and moral outrage.

Returning to *When She Was Good* in 2021, in an America so outwardly different from the one anatomized in Roth's novel, I was taken aback by its relevance to the present. In the portrait of Lucy, with her dogmatic mindset and hardened heart, always the champion of "morality," Roth explores a psychology of personal grievance that resonates eerily on both sides of the political spectrum today. Throughout his career, Roth held true to his injunction to "let the repellent in," which no doubt helps to account for the most common objection to his realism—indeed, to realism itself.[13] As Oscar Wilde said of his own generation, the "dislike of Realism is the rage of Caliban seeing his own face in a glass."[14]

3

The Contemporary Scene in Fiction

In a random selection of popular novels published in the last ten years, I have noticed a curious correspondence: the characters often tend to sound alike. I find myself having to go back and reread dialogue in order to determine who is talking because the speech patterns and even the wit of the characters mirror one another. The idiosyncrasies of speech and manner essential to individuating character in novels of the past are largely absent. Characters speak in a clever, clipped dialogue as if performing on a sitcom, or as if texting had become the model of communication.[1]

This is not always true of course, and it is less true of older writers—for example, Richard Ford, who recently published his fifth novel chronicling the life of Frank Bascombe, *Be Mine* (2023). Bascombe is as complex a character as one could find in a novel by John Updike or, for that matter, George Eliot. But many younger writers do not aim to create complex characters. My two examples of fiction with underdeveloped characters are by well-known and respected contemporary writers. Their novels offer compelling narratives in which each chapter is carefully crafted to build upon the one preceding it. Yet the challenge of developing character is strangely abandoned in these novels. Toward the end of this essay, I will discuss two promising young novelists who depart from this trend.

Our Missing Hearts (2022), a dystopic novel about a Chinese American boy's quest to find his mother, is by Celeste Ng, author of the widely praised *Little Fires Everywhere.*[2] The award-winning *Home Fire* (2017), Kamila Shamsie's seventh novel, is about a Muslim family living in London whose son joins Isis.[3] The plots of *Our Missing Hearts* and *Home Fire* are ingeniously contrived—the latter reads like a political thriller—but the plots don't always gel with the characters. For if character is not sharply defined, action will not be fully realized either or carry much weight. "What is character but the determination of incident? What is incident but the illustration of character?" asked Henry James, echoing one of Aristotle's most basic precepts, that character is action—or, to be more precise, "habitual action."[4] In *The Art of the Novel* (1986) Czech writer Milan Kundera suggested that character is the enduring basis of the novel form.[5] He had in mind avant-garde as well as traditional fiction, for the novelist who experiments with character experiments with form. Kundera himself is a good example of such a novelist, but older examples abound, going back to Laurence Sterne and earlier. The diaries and notes of novelists whom we think of as more mainstream or traditional in their creation of characters—Austen, Dickens, Thackeray, and Hardy, for example—suggest that these writers also began with a particular character when they sat down to write.[6] A well-conceived character engenders the plot or genre that suits it. Austen's Elizabeth Bennet could never thrive in a gothic narrative; we cannot picture Hardy's Jude Fawley making his way over the comic terrain of *Vanity Fair.*[7]

In the contemporary novels mentioned above, however, one senses that the choice of subgenre—dystopia and political thriller—preceded that of character. Ng had already composed a popular novel set in a dystopic suburb. Shamsie was inspired by the Sophocles tragedy, *Antigone*, but upon reading the play, she said, "I knew immediately that I wanted to connect it to a story that was very much in the news at the time, that of young British Muslims and their relationship with the British state."[8] Ng and Shamsie lean heavily on the conventions of subgenre to carry the narrative forward, and the minute particulars that can unite character to action seldom materialize.[9]

Take, for example, the character of the Muslim boy who joins Isis in *Home Fire*. Parvaiz is poor and orphaned. He never knew his father, who was a jihadi terrorist. After his mother dies when he is twelve, Parvaiz is raised by an older sister. He plays videogames, works at a low paying job, and is bullied in the neighborhood. In short, Parvaiz fits the stereotype of a young Muslim man susceptible to recruitment by terrorists: fatherless, poor, and alienated. He has been lifted from the newspapers.

The problem is that Parvaiz's domestic circumstances are at odds with this familiar scenario. Parvaiz is well-loved by the two main characters in *Home Fire*, his older sister Isma and his twin sister Aneeka. Both are gracious presences in his life, as is a neighbor, Aunty Naseem, who lovingly steps in to replace a grandmother when she dies. Aneeka has won a scholarship to the London School of Economics and his older sister is completing a PhD program in sociology in Massachusetts. Parvaiz's academic performance is more average, and although Shamsie hints at his vulnerabilities, he does not strike us as a likely candidate for suicidal derangement. Yet on his first visit to the apartment of the man recruiting him for Isis, he willingly submits to torture, and, on a second visit, asks to be tortured again. Parvaiz is a contrivance used to advance the political plot so that the author can devote her attention to the sisters.

The novel begins with Isma and for the first few chapters we are intrigued by her. A woman torn in many directions, she emerges as a plausible character—that is, as a set of potentialities that promise to unfold over time through the decisions she makes. But Isma drops out of the main action of the novel as the political thriller takes over, as if the author is baffled by the inherent multiplicity she uncovered in the character she has created.

In much fiction today, the idea of *character* is being replaced by a contemporary notion of *agency.* Agency is essentially a political idea that arose in the eighteenth century together with the concept of rights, when belief in human equality started to supplant belief in a natural hierarchy.[10] The idea of agency popular today has the political flavor of the earlier definition and is based on a positive and unitary conception of the self, the self as vessel to be infused with will. Aneeka finally emerges as the heroine of *Home Fire* because she is the strongest agent with the strongest will. Flouting the British government, she goes to the Middle East, claims Parvaiz's dead body after he is murdered, and performs the rituals of mourning. She dies in a terrorist bombing, but she dies heroically, in the act of realizing her will.

The concept of agency inevitably entails a preoccupation with *empowerment.* Since the #MeToo movement emerged, the idea of agency is increasingly associated with the lives of women. An internet entry describes the sense of agency as referring to "the feeling of control over actions and their consequences ....the capacity of women and girls to take purposeful action and pursue goals, free from the threat of violence or retribution. The three core expressions of agency are: decision-making, leadership, and collective action."[11] The root of the word *agent* is the Latin *agentem*, "one who acts," but today's literary concept of agency is more narrow than the traditional idea of action found, for example, in Aristotelian poetics.[12] To Aristotle, action refers to plot, and the main character is the one best fitted to carry it out, whereas today action is understood not in terms of a character's fitness or power to express the depth and variety of an action, but of a character's *control*, or potential control, of an action. Put simply, today's agent is a woman in control in the field of action. When translated to fiction, we see a character who possesses a unitary self acting deliberately and rationally.

Agency is at the heart of the model of empowerment in Ng's *Our Missing Hearts*. Set in a dystopic American city where those of Asian origins are persecuted, the novel tells how Margaret, a Chinese American poet whose work has been banned, must desert her family and disappear altogether in order to save her son Bird from being removed from his household by the state. While in hiding, Margaret takes control of her life by engaging in collective political action, and Bird is eventually empowered to go in search of her when he learns of her plight. Although *Our Missing Hearts* tells the sort of story that reviewers will always refer to as "heartbreaking," its ideological aim is completely rational. *Our Missing Hearts* seeks to enlighten the reader, as the book jacket makes clear, as to "the power—and limitations—of art to create change." In a finger-wagging Author's Note, Ng writes of "the history, in the US and elsewhere, of removing children as a means of political control. If this strikes a nerve with you—and I hope it does—please learn more about the many instances ... in which children have been taken from their families."[13] The sentimental and ideological imperatives of this novel make it impossible for complex characters to emerge. Margaret's function in the novel is simple: she is an agent for political change, and her son's redemptive role is to serve her cause.

It would seem that today political oppression cannot be investigated in a novel without a polemic attached to it, yet this has not always been the case. Kundera's *The Unbearable Lightness of Being* (1984) is set in circumstances more violent and repressive than those described in *Our Missing Hearts.* It takes place mainly in Prague, from the Prague Spring of 1968 to the invasion of Czechoslovakia by the Soviet Union and its aftermath, and it contrasts with *Our Missing Hearts* in that it registers the realistic *inward* impact of fascist politics on the lives of human beings. Unlike the main characters in Ng's novel, Kundera's main characters are not morally pure, they do not become effective political agents, and their inner lives are continually buffeted by the situation in which they live. For example, Tereza becomes preoccupied with her own weakness after her country is invaded: "She was weak ....she was like her country, which stuttered, gasped for breath, could not speak."[14] And when her lover Tomas finds himself in a situation where he must decide whether to collaborate with the Soviet authorities, his colleagues' cynical interest in what he will do completely unnerves him. "He was surprised at ... how panic-stricken [their interest] made him feel."[15] It is the behavior of his colleagues toward him, none of whom has the slightest intention of standing up to the authorities themselves that prompts him to refuse to collaborate. What distinguishes Tomas and Tereza from others in the novel is that, to them, the "truth" is not manifest. Their own and others' intentions are always open to question. The characters in *Our Missing Hearts* are immune to the kind of intimate derailment Kundera's characters suffer because they are empowered by an idea of "truth." Kundera's novels are full of minor characters who fit this description, of course, but his major characters overshadow them with their human indecision and lack of certainty. When we go inside the head of a Kundera character, we find multiplicity, not unity. We encounter contradiction, dynamic movement, change, and flux.

A finely drawn character evolves gradually in the course of a narrative, distinguishing itself by means of decisions or actions, whereas an author overcommitted to the notion of agency tends to produce static or reduced images of human life, the most extreme example being the paradigmatic "agent" of Ian Fleming's novels, James Bond, that master of technological devices. When the contrivances of plot overdetermine character, as in the character of Parvaiz, we may still learn something about the world we live in, but the potential of the novel to teach us anything about the individual self disintegrates.

Tellingly, both Ng and Shamsie are entranced by technology and display their characters' cleverness in mastering their devices or in producing witty text messages, as if texting were the most expressive, instead of the most diminished, form of communication available to us. In *Our Missing Hearts*, Margaret's great achievement is to put her protest into action by means of a computer program that broadcasts audio to each of the thousands of bottle caps she has planted around the city. Pedestrians returning home from work are forced to listen as she reads heartfelt narratives of displaced children into a microphone, her voice resounding across the city through the network of bottlecaps. The protest is intended to symbolize the power of art to bring about change, as Ng's allusions to Anna Akmatova, the patron saint of her novel, make clear. Instead (to this reader at least), the scene eerily recalls Mao's compulsory broadcasts from radios installed in houses during the Cultural Revolution. While Ng may have intended the scene to signify her character's apotheosis as an artist, the action of the novel communicates something very different: the subordination of art in the service of politics and technology.

Shamsie's romance with technology is more furtive. In *Home Fire*, the final scene of immolation is shown on international TV where it is endlessly replayed, an image of life at a remove, of life (literally) mediated. It has been said that, when we read the great works of realist fiction of the nineteenth century, we feel as though we can reach out and touch the characters. That is not remotely possible in Shamsie's final scene. A shadow falls between the image of Aneeka's immolation and the reader's apprehension of it: call it technology. We may as well be watching the scene on TV.

Of course not every young writer participates in the trend to embrace the idea of agency. Morgan Talty's *The Night of the Living Rez* (2022) brings us much closer to the lives of its characters than the contemporary novels discussed above. Set on a Penobscot reservation in Maine, it is made up of a series of interconnected stories that follow the growth of a boy named Dee. The natural world comes to life in Talty's writing; even a porcupine has personality. The characters' lives are intertwined with the earth, not simply because of their poverty or a tribal identification with the land, but because Talty understands them as biological creatures living in time. Characters appear and then reappear in a later story, changed and often damaged by what they have lived through, yet we recognize them as we would members of our own family.

A chapter titled "Get Me Some Medicine" begins: "A November rain battered the window above the kitchen sink, and a damp brown leaf pressed against the glass."[16] Dee and his friend Fellis play poker at the kitchen table. A few weeks earlier Fellis had dropped out of community college, which he claims to have attended for only three weeks to get a refund check from financial aid. Near the end of the story we learn that Fellis had taken a philosophy class, trying to understand it, until he discovered that in the opening lectures the instructor was not talking about Aeropostale, a clothing brand, but "some guy named Aristotle." "For fuck's sake," Fellis tells his mother, "I didn't belong there."[17]

Fellis and Dee talk in a friendly, defensive, random way, laughing and arguing. They decide to go out to a bar and after several drinks run into Meekaw, whom Fellis intensely dislikes because he believes Meekaw cheated him when he bought a bag of coke from him. Meekaw is younger than Fellis and has done well at the university, attaining Dean's List, and gaining recognition in the tribal paper. Having sold drugs to help pay his car loan, he is now saving up for medical school. We are only a few pages into the story, and Talty has already given us three finely etched characters. All are Native-American men in their twenties, but the differences among them in speech, manner, intelligence, and awareness are firmly established.

The three men leave the bar together and enter a wood. Increasingly drunk, Fellis begins to press Meekaw for coke. "Fellis drank the tall boy and then he shone the phone's light in Meekaw's face. He squinted, and like the squirrel he was named after, Meekaw had no indent between the bridge of his nose up to his brow."[18] Fellis accuses Meekaw of cheating him in the past and a fight ensues. Meekaw is smaller than Fellis but wiry and agile, and when Fellis, losing the fight, shouts that he is being stabbed with a knife, Dee comes to his aid, striking Meekaw on the top of his skull with a bag of heavy cans of beer. Meekaw falls face down in the mud, then rolls onto his back holding his head. Fellis kicks the ground over Meekaw's body and the men leave.

Later, after Dee learns that Fellis lied about the knife, he returns to the wood and is relieved to find that "Meekaw is gone, but an imprint of where he'd been remained in the mud next to the river, and the great heap of earth Fellis had covered him with was scattered about. I wondered how long it would stay that way."[19] Did Meekaw depart without serious injury or did he crawl away like a wounded animal? And is Dee wondering how long the evidence of the crime will remain or how long the presence of human life will endure on the reservation? Dee's developing consciousness contains a fledgling conscience. Finally losing his temper with Fellis, he breaks his nose, but in a later chapter, now aware that Fellis is mentally ill, he accompanies Fellis to the hospital for ECT treatment, walking up the steps with him even though he is aware Fellis doesn't need his help. Nature—human and material—repairs her ravages.

Like Kundera's people, Talty's characters reveal themselves in countless infinitesimal details, such that any summary of the action feels ham-handed. They possess an unaccountable vitality. The reader does not contemplate them at a respectable distance or entertain abstract political remedies for their impossibly difficult lives. We experience what they experience. To speak of agency in relation to a character like Fellis is absurd, and not because agency is irrelevant to his life or that of other characters in *The Night of the Living Rez.* Meekaw, Fellis's mother Beth, and other characters seek control in dealing with their circumstances. But at any given moment in the life of a character, the question of agency is not the only or even the most important question that Talty puts before us. The porcupine clinging to the top of a tree, as it looks down in fear at the human beings trying to trap it, reflects the state of mind of many of Talty's characters, living with the possible demise of their community.[20]

Since Talty himself grew up on a Penobscot reservation in Maine, it's not surprising that he has been assigned the role of Indigenous writer. The *New York Times* declares that Talty "has assured himself a spot in the canon of Native-American literature."[21] I believe such praise is justified, yet it might also be said that Talty takes his place in a tradition of North American literature about rural and small town life that stretches from Sherwood Anderson and Willa Cather to the Southern Gothic writers and on up to John Updike's Olinger stories and the work of Alice Munro. Placing Talty's work in that tradition does not diminish his importance as a Native-American writer; it serves as a reminder of the long shadow cast by the tradition of fiction, and of the centrality of character to its development.

Writers like Talty with the ability to create complex characters exist, but reviewers for the well-known venues today and judges of literary prizes do not always point us to them. When it comes to reviewer selection, sensationalistic subject matter usually wins the day. What attracts reviewers to Shamsie's, Ng's, and even Talty's fiction, it would seem, has been the socio-political relevance of their subjects more than the power of their characters to bring the socio-political situation to life.[22]

Even Colm Tóibín's *The Magician* (2021), a work that attempts to recreate the famously complex personality of Thomas Mann, succumbs to a reductive view of character.[23] Tóibín knows very well that he has chosen a multifaceted person to portray, and he wisely does not embrace a unitary conception of Mann's self, but neither does he pursue an idea of the self as manifold. Tóibín's Mann is a duality: there is the respectably married author and the repressed homosexual. Mann is a failed agent in *The Magician*; he fails to act on his homosexuality, and he therefore comes across as a slightly pathetic figure.

By tying Mann to this formula, Tóibín chose to underplay an important strain in Mann's character—his astonishing *lack* of insecurity about his sexuality. Mann made no serious attempt to hide the fascination he felt for attractive young men from his wife Katia (to whom he was happily married for fifty years), or even from his adult children, nor was he concerned about the conclusion readers would draw from *Death in Venice*, which is about an older man's fascination with a beautiful young boy. What does this tell us about Mann? Not that he was a "closeted gay man," as Tóibín characterized him in interviews, but a cosmopolitan, possibly omnisexual, artist, an *unfixed* self.[24]

In listening to interviews with Tóibín, Talty, Ng, and Shamsie, I have been struck by how much pressure is put on writers to reduce *themselves* to a fixed identity, or to speak authoritatively from personal experience about their novel's subject. Thus Tóibín, who is gay, is called upon to speak from personal knowledge of his sense of Mann as a closeted gay man, and Talty speaks of his experiences growing up on a Penobscot reservation. Yet Tóibín does not use the term "closeted gay man" to describe Mann in *The Magician*, only in interviews, and Talty, in one interview, mentions that it was not until he abandoned memoir-writing that his work took flight. In interviews Ng and Shamsie seem reluctant to label themselves Asian-American or Muslim writers—allowing oneself to be seen, or to see oneself, as representative of an entire ethnic population or oppressed class is, to say the least, risky. It may help to sell novels but it also leads readers, reviewers, and even authors themselves to oversimplify novels and reduce characters to types.

In a letter to A.S. Suvorin in 1888, Anton Chekhov wrote the following:

> It is time for writers … to admit that you can't figure out anything in this world, as Socrates once admitted and as Voltaire kept admitting. The public thinks it knows and understands everything; and the dumber it is the broader its horizons seem to be. However, if an artist whom the public believes decides to state that he understands nothing of what he sees, that in itself is of great significance in the realm of thought and is a great step forward.[25]

The public that "thinks it knows and understands everything" sounds rather like the present-day public. And to an even greater extent than in Chekhov's day, people get their ideas not from observing life, but from the media. Today, this includes not only newspapers but the internet and social media. When people either like a novel they have read or think they might like to read one, they search out interviews with the author on the internet. What if authors were more honest about stating that they understand "nothing of what they see"? In Tóibín's many interviews, he readily gives the interviewer what the interviewer often hungers for: information on Mann as a "closeted gay man" by the author who had once been closeted. In a more serious interview with Christopher Lydon, however, Tóibín remarks on Mann's "ghostly presence" as an artist, his unknowability as a subject.[26]

Chekhov's letter suggests that the artist's power lies in "what he sees," not in what he "understands." The artist's obligation is to present the world through his vision, not to pontificate about it in interviews or through ideologically determined characters. When the public "believes" an artist, the public is openly declaring its dependence on that vision, its grateful reliance on the artist's unique ability to help it see the world anew.

For better or worse, character is essential to the novelist's vision. One of the most powerful examples of this principle may be found in the celebrated experimental novel by Patricia Lockwood, *No One Is Talking about This* (2021). Lacking both plot and character, the first sections of the novel are narrated by a nameless woman who is almost always online, endlessly scrolling and ultimately trapped inside a virtual platform she calls "the portal."[27] We come to know her random thoughts and to pick up random details about her travels, her husband, and her original family, but she does not emerge as a character until she learns her sister is carrying a child with a rare condition that is likely to cause the death of the child soon after birth. When she and her family receive the brutal shock of the tragedy, *No One Is Talking about This* shifts from being a collection of observations to a novel. The narrator stops gawking and starts to see, and the narrative begins to show faith in the value of human life and to register the weight of human choices. The dying infant plays a significant role here. She too is a character and the narrator speculates on what might happen when, after her death, the doctors harvest her brain: "as long as people were looking at that mind, it was still active in the world, asking and answering, finding out about things, making small dear cries of discovery."[28]

No One Is Talking about This is composed of disconnected paragraphs, each separated from the one preceding it by a line space. It reads like a list of unrelated thoughts and impressions reminiscent of the aphoristic styles of Wilde and Nietzsche, but whereas in the earlier authors, the style announced a refusal to adhere to any system, Lockwood's narrator is the willing disciple of a new technology of unlimited distractions. On lecture tour in Vienna, swinging in the highest car of the Ferris wheel in the Prater, she is finally borne out of the portal; her phone rings and she hears her mother's voice, "Something has gone wrong … How soon can you get here?"[29] Lockwood's experiment in form, then, rises directly out of the giddy character she has created. The woman seems incapable of connected thought until a plot suddenly emerges that weaves her disparate impressions and speculations together.

Earlier, at the height of her passionate engagement with the internet—"a warm body that wanted her"—she learns of foreign attacks on the nation's infrastructure and of the widespread surveillance of devices taking place.[30] Feeling undefended and panicked, she imagines what people in the future will know about her generation: "You will be so wise!" she exclaims with bitter irony. "You will understand everything about our time! And you will know nothing about us!"[31] It is as if the narrator, who is a writer, is finally awakening to the tacit obligations of fiction-writing.

PART TWO

CHARACTER IN ITS MORAL CONTEXT

4

"How Pleasant It Is to Have Money, Heigh Ho!"

In America today, the acquisition of wealth is widely regarded as a desirable end in itself. By "wealth" I mean an excess of money and possessions—more than enough to live comfortably. Even allowing for different degrees and definitions of comfort, there is a clear divide between a life in which some degree of monetary vigilance is required for survival and one in which such vigilance is not a concern. Many people in our society strive for wealth, or fantasize about possessing it, with a naivete that their ancestors would have wondered at.

In earlier periods in history, suspicion of the alleged benefits of wealth was more pervasive than it is today because religious denunciations of greed were commonplace. Medieval concepts of usury lingered in the cultural consciousness, as did Aristotle's distinction between "wealth-getting," or the pursuit of infinite profit, and household economy, in which money is a means to an end different from money.[1] Most people would have known the lines from Matthew 19:24, when Jesus states firmly, "And again I say unto you, It is easier for a camel to go through the eye of a needle, than for a rich man to enter into the kingdom of God." They would have been familiar with Timothy 6:7: "For we brought nothing into this world, and it is certain we can carry nothing out."

According to Max Weber, however, the pursuit of wealth and possessions received a considerable boost in religious support during the seventeenth century when capitalism arose in Northern Europe. In his famous 1904 essay, "The Protestant Ethic and the Spirit of Capitalism," Weber argued that capitalism did not emerge before the seventeenth century because, up until then, most people were contented to work only for what they needed to maintain their station in life. For example, agricultural records show that if landowners offered workers more money during the gathering of the harvest, so as to bolster productivity during a critical period of time, laborers "reacted to the increase not by increasing but by decreasing the amount of [their] work."[2] Workers sought only to earn what they had earned before to take care of their traditional needs. But in the seventeenth century earning money became a moral good. This happened because of the rise of what Weber refers to as "ascetic Protestantism," or religious ideas rooted in the work of Martin Luther and especially John Calvin. In their view, salvation was predestined, but those who *lived* as though they were among the elect—through hard work and the acquisition of wealth—could be confident they were among the chosen. The pursuit of wealth with a clear conscience became easier, marking a development in culture that provided novelists with ample opportunity to explore the inherent contradictions of life in a predominantly Christian and capitalist society.

The first English novel, Daniel Defoe's *Robinson Crusoe* (1719), was published in the period when capitalism arose, and it registers these contradictions with extraordinary clarity. The restless, acquisitive young Crusoe, who is bent on seeing the world, has numerous adventures, including being taken as a slave in Morocco. With the assistance of a boy named Xury, he escapes slavery, only to subsequently sell Xury himself into slavery, with the proviso that Xury be set free after ten years if he becomes a Christian. Later, while on an illegal expedition to purchase slaves in Africa, Crusoe's ship is wrecked and, as we know, he finds himself stranded on a desert island for twenty-eight years.

In his struggle to survive on the island, Crusoe ransacks the ship for goods, building up a huge stock of objects, only a fraction of which he will ever use. The reader does not pause to wonder whether or not storing fifteen great wicker baskets in his small cave dwelling makes sense because Defoe has placed his hero in the ideal situation for a *surplus* to seem a *necessity*.[3] In a famous moment in the narrative, Crusoe discovers some money in a locker on board the ship, loudly laments its uselessness to him, and then pockets it anyway.

Defoe's ambivalent portrait of the pursuit of wealth reverberates throughout English fiction. In any given genre, writers build on earlier writers, offering new answers to questions earlier writers have posed. As readers, we benefit just as much from the wisdom that emerges from a tradition as from individual works. So, what does the English novel tradition teach us about the effects of wealth on human character?

Few bodies of literature offer a more thorough critique of the impact of money on the lives of human beings than the Victorian novel.[4] This is not surprising, given that England was the first country in the world to become industrialized and therefore the wealthiest country in the world throughout the nineteenth century. If you want to know what the desire for money can do to people, and what the possession of large amounts of money often does to people's character, begin by reading Austen, who died less than two years before Queen Victoria's birth in 1819, and follow with pretty much any major novelist coming after her: Dickens, Charlotte and Emily Brontë, Thackeray, Trollope, Hardy, and Forster, who considered himself a kind of "last Victorian." The social vision of each of these writers extends beyond the operation of money to include many other forces—individual and communal, political and historical, natural and supernatural—but money's influence is rarely ignored. Even the ghosts in Victorian fiction cannot withstand its effects, as anyone knows who has seen film adaptations of Dickens during the holiday season.[5]

All the novelists mentioned above acknowledge "how pleasant it is to have money," as Victorian poet A.H. Clough put it in a well-known satiric poem.[6] Austen and Dickens tend to reward their heroes and heroines with extreme wealth, but the prize does not come until the characters prove they are not (or no longer) susceptible to being corrupted by it. They must first achieve knowledge of themselves and of the workings of money in society. Notably, however, in Austen's last novel, *Persuasion* (1817), and in Dickens's late and most famous novel, *Great Expectations* (1861), the main characters find themselves in relatively insecure circumstances compared to what their earlier, less mature selves desired. Anne Elliot's husband, despite his money, may face another military engagement, and Pip is not rewarded with the dizzying inheritance he had hoped for. The enthusiasm of both authors for the reward of riches appears to have cooled.

In the early fiction of Austen and Dickens, remnants of the classical idea of the potential virtue of the wealthy may be seen. Both authors would have known the *Nicomachean Ethics,* in which Aristotle identifies the necessary virtue of the rich as that of "magnificence," or what today we might call philanthropy. These worthy rich people spend their money "for honour's sake" on aesthetically beautiful and morally beneficial projects and gifts that benefit the public.[7] In *Pride and Prejudice* (1813), Darcy's responsible management of the Pemberley estate and the beauty of the estate itself are signs of his virtue. Pickwick's generosity in spending the fortune he made in business in *Pickwick Papers* (1837) and the Cheeryble brothers' philanthropy in *Nicholas Nickleby* (1839) are examples of virtuous magnificence from Dickens's early novels.

In much of Austen's fiction, however, rich people who live on fortunes they did nothing to produce (and are doing much to reduce) are consistently satirized for their complacency, stupidity, or self-deception. Many such characters, like the selfish, narrow-minded Bingley sisters or the coarse Lady Catherine de Bourgh in *Pride and Prejudice*, are memorably exposed. But it is in the wealthy characters we either like, or grow to like, that we see Austen's most extended investigations into the effects of money on character. In the first half of *Pride and Prejudice,* Darcy is arrogant, proud, and insulting to the heroine. His education and intelligence do not protect him from the damage to moral character that consciousness of wealth and privilege can inflict. It is only after he falls in love with the heroine, Elizabeth Bennet, that he begins to see himself clearly, or to recognize that being a good man in theory is not the same as being a good man in practice. As he later tells Elizabeth, he had been given sound principles, but was left to follow them in pride and conceit. Happily born into a high position, he had been cosseted, praised, and deferred to, and he therefore grew up to be, at times, as insensible of his effect on others as his pompous aunt, Lady Catherine—until he meets Elizabeth.

Few characters in Austen's novels escape being morally diminished by material wealth. The lethal combination may be wealth mixed with other "blessings," like good looks and intelligence, but it is wealth that gives the other advantages their force in society. "Handsome, clever, and rich" Emma Woodhouse, the heroine of *Emma* (1816), had been raised "with very little to distress or vex her" and consequently acquired a disposition to think very highly of herself.[8] Wealth, looks, brains—this three-fold blessing or blight is largely responsible for Emma's habitual complacency and her unconscious cruelty to two people: a socially vulnerable young woman who happens to enter her midst, and whom Emma maneuvers into a disastrous misjudgment of the heart, and a kindly, plain older woman living in genteel poverty whom Emma humiliates in the presence of others. One woman lacks brains, the other, youth and looks, but what they most crucially do without is the protective status that money provides.

On any list of vices, complacency—which Victorian novelists consistently associated with the possession of wealth—is not likely to rank very high. It is not included among the seven deadly sins, for example. But whereas people can easily recognize lust, gluttony, and wrath in themselves, they may be too complacent in their complacency to recognize its typical manifestations: preening, condescension to others, and close-mindedness—all tendencies that are deadly enough in their own right, and deadening to the spirit of the person who indulges them.

As Victorian fiction develops, the critique of financial capitalism grows stronger. Emphasis shifts from focus on the consequences of individual greed to systemic evils, especially in Dickens's late novels. But novelistic interest in wealth's impact on individual human character never lets up. In Thackeray and Dickens, a common fault of the person who, lacking money, desperately desires and finally acquires it, is a tendency to betray himself in addition to betraying others. As soon as young Pip comes into a sudden, mysterious fortune in Dickens's *Great Expectations* (1861), separation between him and those who love him sets in. At the moment the gift is announced, Pip is so overjoyed that he doesn't even notice that Joe Gargery, the blacksmith who adopted him as a child, is immobilized by sorrow at the prospect of losing his young friend. Pip condescends to his neighbor Biddy, who earlier taught him to read, and he forms a plan to benefit his hometown once he is settled in London by bestowing "a pint of ale, and a gallon of condescension, upon everybody in the village."[9]

As if anaesthetized by his sense of superiority, Pip is embarrassed by Joe's awkward manners and inferior dress when Joe visits him in the city; he proves incapable of receiving the blacksmith in a forthright way. Only after Pip learns that his money did not come from a respectable source does he begin to see clearly and regret what he has done. Joe remains unchanged in his feelings, demonstrating what Dickens calls, with beautiful irony, "the wealth of his great nature."[10] It is Pip who has changed, and who finally realizes that there is no going back. "The change was made in me; the thing was done."[11]

To the largely Protestant society of the Victorians, the possibility of irrevocable inner loss was among the terrors of the moral life, as disturbing to them as reading Dante's *Inferno* must have been to medieval Catholics. If, to today's secular reader, Clough's jingle sounds like no more than a comic acknowledgment of the truth, to many Victorians it would have left a bitter taste.

They may talk as they please about what they call pelf,
And how one ought never to think of one's self,
And how pleasures of thought surpass eating and drinking–
My pleasure of thought is the pleasure of thinking
How pleasant it is to have money, heigh ho!
How pleasant it is to have money.[12]

Today *pelf* means money or riches, but it was originally associated with stolen goods and has always had negative connotations. Clough's rhyme insultingly links *pelf* with the avaricious *self.*

In comparison with Austen and Dickens, Trollope communicates a more consistent perspective on the dangers that wealth poses to human character. It's true that the "good life," a term that appears in Trollope's Barsetshire series, has a decidedly materialistic flavor in his novels. Trollope knows very well the roots of the concept of the Good Life in Plato's *Phaedrus,* and he tracks an essentially Platonic progress toward virtue, wisdom, and knowledge in the lives of his main characters more doggedly than the novelists mentioned above. But the "good life" that Trollope has in mind for his characters is not a wealthy life. It is life in a comfortable, nicely furnished house, with good food, companionship, and a loving family. The impoverished, "good" man in Trollope's novels, however virtuous and wise, suffers irreparably from his privations, but the wealthy person who allows money values to master him or her is impoverished in another way; more often than not, wealthy characters possess an abundance of charm but "no real feeling."[13] Embracing a classical ideal of moderation, Trollope's conception of the good life often represents a fruitful mean between wealth and poverty.

Published in 1910, less than a decade after Queen Victoria's death, Forster's *Howards End* boldly extends earlier novelists' critique of money values, and ends by affirming a Trollopian moderation. At the beginning of *Howards End*, the heroine Margaret Schlegel and her sister Helen are given a taste of the pleasures of wealth when they rub shoulders with the Wilcox family, most of whose members are so jolly and self-satisfied that they could be chanting Clough's rhyme under their breath. But Helen's momentary love affair with the younger son Paul ends in disaster, and Margaret's eventual marriage to the widowed father Henry almost dissolves when his hypocrisy and heartlessness are exposed. By the novel's end, Margaret's humane values prevail, Henry is chastened, and they settle into a modest, contented existence with Helen and her illegitimate child. In a final scene we learn that Margaret has asked Henry to exclude her from his will and that she plans to give away most of her own money during her lifetime. Private tragedies and public humiliations are necessary before this highly unconventional ending unfolds, and in showing the reader all the reasons why it is the most fulfilling conclusion for Margaret and Henry, Forster does not reject money per se; he demystifies it. Money will continue to play a necessary role in their domestic lives, but the Wilcox pursuit of wealth for its own sake and on a grand scale, which included profiting from imperialist enterprises, has come to an end, together with the family's habit of organizing their personal lives around getting and spending. Their *experience* of life has changed.

It took a century, then, for the novelists of an immensely rich country to demystify the attractions of wealth. And, like Forster in *Howards End*, modernist writers such as Lawrence and Conrad accomplished their own demystifications by means of broad critiques of English civilization—that is, by representing wealth not as a reward for the virtuous but as part of a global system of capitalist exploitation. As naïve as the old narratives of reward and punishment may seem to us today, these earlier narratives forged the connection between human character and economic reality without which later fiction writers would not have been able even to think about questions of social justice. For what Austen, Dickens, Trollope, and other novelists show is that, before matters of economic justice can be addressed, a morally developed individual must exist to address them.

5

The Singular Happiness of the Artist

Suffering sells. According to executives at the tabloid magazine *National Enquirer*, nothing can drive up sales more than a cover that includes the words “sad last days.” While the literati may not purchase tabloids at the checkout counter of supermarkets, they are not immune to the attraction of tales of suffering, especially in the lives of artists. The biographical legacy of Oscar Wilde, the first of several writers discussed in this essay, has been overdetermined by the trials he endured. The Romantic poets, in whom the myth of the suffering artist originated, preceded Wilde, but the sad circumstances of his life gave the myth added momentum. Wilde was sentenced to two years of hard labor for homosexual acts, a punishment notorious for its brutality. He died at the age of forty-six, two years after his release from prison.

The story of Wilde’s disgrace is not all there is to the story of his life. The life-affirming qualities of his character call into question the tendency today to see the life of the homosexual artist as prone to misery. Given that Wilde did indeed suffer at the hands of English law, it is easy to forget that he possessed to the end of his life an unusually playful temperament and often expressed amusement over the vagaries of human existence, including his own. Wilde once said that he lived in fear of being understood. It turns out he had reason to fear. The legal charges against him resulted in his being "understood," in the late nineteenth and early twentieth centuries, as the evil seducer of a pure and innocent young man—a judgment that borders on the comical when one considers the life and character of Wilde's lover, Lord Alfred Douglas. (In Richard Ellmann's splendid biography of Wilde, Douglas emerges as one of the most dissolute young men of his day.[1]) In our own time, Wilde is "understood" by means of another stereotype: that of the victimized gay artist.

My intention is not to minimize the victimization that did take place. Wilde's literary reputation was immediately compromised when he was arrested. During the trials, his name was removed from the marquee at theaters where his plays were being performed, and publication of the full text of *De Profundis*, a memoir he wrote while in prison, was delayed until 1949. But Wilde's works have survived, and have long been widely respected. It makes sense, then, to consider whether doubly encasing his personal life in popular myth—the myth of the suffering artist and the myth of the damaged homosexual—is helpful in understanding the highly original personality behind such brilliant work. Whatever Wilde may have suffered, his character and creativity appear to have been sufficiently buoyant to navigate a sea of troubles.

Wilde was born in 1854 into an intellectual and cosmopolitan family in Dublin. From an early age he was at home in the artistic, bohemian, and aristocratic circles in which his parents moved, where homosexuality was not a pressing concern, let alone the guilt-ridden bogey it was to the middle classes. In researching Wilde's life some years ago for a book on his critical and philosophical writings, I could find no evidence that he experienced guilt about his sexual desires.[2] In *De Profundis*, he suggests that he found his lover's need to talk endlessly about the subject of homosexuality tedious.

Wilde enjoyed pulling the rug out from under anyone's belief in an elementary or essential identity. Insincerity, he often suggested, is merely augmentation of personality. He did not identify as a homosexual per se—the word homosexual itself did not enter the language until the late nineteenth century—and his sexual history suggests a characteristically Wildean inconsistency. He was happily married to Constance Lloyd until, at the age of thirty-four, he began a relationship with his friend and later editor, Robert Ross. There is some evidence that when Wilde later became interested in the underworld of homosexual prostitution, he did so in order to live out the critique of convention that we see in his writings as much as to satisfy his desires. "How I used to toy with that tiger Life!" he wrote to a friend.[3]

Given Wilde's penchant for contradiction, it is not surprising that, despite his rejection of the idea of a fixed identity, he very clearly identified himself as an artist. But when he writes of identity in *De Profundis*, he moves beyond subjectivist psychology toward a metaphysical conception associated with art and memory. The "spiritual singularity of artists sets them socially apart, in the long run, whether they are sexual 'outsiders' or not," writes Helen Vendler.[4] My book on Wilde's philosophy of art explores this "spiritual singularity," whereas here, my focus is on Wilde's character, especially on what William Butler

Yeats described as the "dominating self-possession" of his personality in the face of disaster.[5]

From all reports, Wilde was a magnanimous man, and continued to be so to the end, despite the fact that many friends dropped him when he was put on trial, and few fellow artists signed petitions for mitigation of a sentence widely known to result in death. When he learned that some of the most damning clues in the case against him were provided by an entirely voluntary agent, an actor named Charles Brookfield whom Wilde was known to have helped, Wilde said, "How absurd of Brookfield!"[6]

Although Wilde's health deteriorated in prison, his spirit remained strong. He made friends there and did all he could on behalf of imprisoned children, whose weeping he could hear from inside his cell. In a note to a prison warder with whom he became friends, he wrote: "Please find out for me the name of A.2.11. Also: the names of the children who are in for the rabbits; and the amount of the fine .... Can I pay this and get them out?"[7] Wilde was bankrupted at this point and had little money to spare.

Two years after his release from prison, ill and dying in Paris, Wilde uttered one of his most famous witticisms. Alluding to the ugly wallpaper in his hotel room, he mordantly remarked that he knew "one or the other of us would have to go."[8] Wilde's internal aplomb is always evident in his wit; here it is proof of his lack of self-pity, a quality that may also be seen in more serious statements. A few months before his death he encountered an old friend of his mother's, Comtesse Anna de Brémont, who had found it necessary to cut him at a café the day before, only, to her relief, to run into him the next day on a passenger steamer on the Seine. Characteristically, Wilde admonishes her: "Life held to my lips a full flavoured cup and I drank it to the dregs … Contessa, don't sorrow for me."[9]

Wilde continued to write, and to experience joy in writing, as long as his health permitted. The categorical view of his life as one of persecution and suffering is belied by Wilde's letters, notebooks, and diaries, and by the record of his creative achievement. His story should make us all the more suspicious of popular interpretations of artists' lives that flourish when letters, diaries, and works have been lost. Such was the case in the story I am about to tell.

It has been said that the death of a beautiful woman is the essence of romantic tragedy. If we add to this notion the myth of the suffering artist—especially the suffering woman artist—and throw into the mix the Victorian myth of the fallen woman, we arrive at the popular conception of the life of Mary Ellen Meredith.

Mary Ellen is mainly known, if she is known at all, for being the adulterous first wife of the famous novelist and poet George Meredith. She published very little during her short life and died before realizing her ambitions as a writer, leaving behind only a handful of articles, including essays on "Death" and "Gastronomy and Civilisation," and some poems. We know that Meredith published some of her poems under his own name and that she and Meredith collaborated in composing other poems. According to the stage drama most Victorians believed, Mary Ellen fell passionately in love with the painter Henry Wallis and rashly left her husband to live with him. She disgraced herself further by having an illegitimate child. Like many a fallen woman in novels and plays, she was cruelly abandoned by her lover and shunned by all, including her own family. Forced to live in destitute circumstances, she eventually, so the story goes, took her own life, like the figure of the adulterous wife in Meredith's greatest poem, *Modern Love*. *Modern Love* became Mary Ellen's epitaph. Most people who recognize her name know of her because of this poem, and do not distinguish between the figure in the poem and Mary Ellen herself.

Through painstaking research, Diane Johnson, author of *The True History of the First Mrs. Meredith and Other Lesser Lives*, uncovered a more accurate account. Her trenchant, elegantly written book was first published in 1972 but fell into obscurity, perhaps because its portrait of Mrs. Meredith did not conform to either a narrative of female victimization or one of soaring triumph-over-tragedy. In 2020, the book was reissued as a New York Review of Books Classic.

Mary Ellen, the brilliant oldest child of the writer Thomas Love Peacock, was educated to think for herself. The worldly Peacock, who associated with unconventional and intellectual women all his life, gave his favorite child free rein in his household on the River Thames, where she grew up well-acquainted with writers and artists. She married at twenty-two, but her husband drowned three months later in a gale while attempting to rescue a sailor, leaving her a widow in 1844. She had already become pregnant.

Far from seeking help at this time, Mary Ellen was eager to live independently. When her father made plans to visit her after her husband's death, she begged him not to come. She wanted to manage on her own and had plans to support herself as a writer. When circumstances eventually became too difficult, however, she returned home with her child.

Mary Ellen met George Meredith in 1848. He immediately fell in love with her, and together they began editing a literary magazine. She was seven years older than Meredith and, according to several accounts, possessed a masterful personality. She was also beautiful and witty, and not eager to remarry. Meredith had to propose to her six times before she finally accepted.

Mary Ellen conceived two children with Meredith, both of whom died in childbirth, possibly causing or aggravating the disease of the kidneys that would eventually kill her. After giving birth to a son who survived, she and Meredith grew apart and, having always been intellectually independent, she decided to leave him. Although we do not know when she became lovers with Henry Wallis (who was nine years her junior), it seems that the actual circumstances of her decision to leave Meredith may have been unrelated to Wallis. "Mary Ellen simply left George, intending to live by her writing and a small private income. Her involvement with Henry was not necessarily even related to her separation from George," writes Johnson.[10]

Mary Ellen seems to have had the same view of marriage as that of her father's old friend Percy Shelley, who believed that a husband and wife should continue together only so long as they loved each other and should not allow the law to determine matters of human affection. She did not seem to care about public opinion, nor did her father, who continued to write to her in a chatty vein as she attempted to earn money as a writer. She gave birth to a child, fathered by Wallis, but there appears to have been no secrecy in her family about it. Peacock wrote cheerfully to his old friend Claire Clairmont about the little boy. (Claire had had a child out of wedlock herself, fathered by

Lord Byron.) Mary Ellen enjoyed being a mother and named her love child Felix, which means happiness.

Eventually Mary Ellen became too ill to write and at times may have had difficulty collecting what was owed to her. A letter from Dickens seems to be asking a friend to contact George Meredith about where to send compensation for something Mary Ellen had published in Dickens's magazine. Under the law, husbands had a right to their wives' income, as they did to custody of children. Meredith refused to allow Mary Ellen to see her son, although she managed to do so through the clandestine efforts of friends.

We know from letters discovered by Johnson that Mary Ellen was together with Wallis for periods and also separated from him. Their correspondence suggests a friendship as well as a love relationship. Her tone is "equable and independent," perhaps in consequence of an understanding between them to impose no obligations.[11] She wrote to Wallis for advice about her writing and confided in him her fears that her intelligence would be swallowed up by her long illness. As death approached, she accepted her fate, was cared for by friends, and did not, contrary to myth, either kill herself or die alone and in squalid circumstances. Her father, who never recovered from his grief, remained lifelong friends with Henry Wallis. Evidently, Peacock detested George Meredith.

Once the various myths—wicked woman, abandoned woman—are dispelled, we can appreciate the spirit of a gifted person who tried, against great odds, to develop her artistic talent. Like Wilde, Mary Ellen suffered as all human beings suffer, but, like Wilde again, she did not suffer the way conventional persons suffer when they go against convention. She identified not with the mainstream of society but with the milieu of artists and writers she had known since childhood. She suffered as an artist when circumstances or ill health prevented her from writing. The cheap melodrama imposed on her life by the popular imagination marks an effort to make her character recognizable to the average Victorian. The public wants Life to imitate Art, but Life—"poor, probable, uninteresting human life" as Wilde called it—is woefully lacking in form.[12]

Biographers can sometimes reclaim a life held hostage to the myth of the suffering artist if the artist lived long enough to overcome disability and pain. Sarah Bernhardt, Arthur Rimbaud, and Carson McCullers are examples. If we see gender as a disability, which it was for writers in the nineteenth century, Charlotte Brontë and George Eliot offer more examples. Both novelists surmounted discouragement and self-suppression, and were acclaimed while they were still living. But Oscar Wilde and Mary Ellen Meredith died relatively young, and they died soon enough after their difficulties for misfortune to define them in the public eye. That was not how they defined themselves. Both continued to create despite personal losses and upheavals. In the period leading up to Wilde's trial, which was also the period of his greatest creativity, he went on holiday in Algiers, where he said to a friend, "The sun is jealous of art."[13]

The myth of the suffering artist not only can blind us to facts about the artist's life and personality; it can distort our expectations about the work. Authors who lived to write about their experience in concentration camps during the Second World War have often felt prohibited from writing about anything else. The Italian writer Primo Levi achieved worldwide fame for his 1947 *Survival in Auschwitz* and, in the eyes of many, came to be viewed as a "Jewish saint." Aware that producing stories on other subjects would be "viewed as an abdication," he published his first non-Holocaust book in 1966 under a pseudonym.[14] Reviewers were not pleased, but were made happy again when he returned to the subject of the war in *The Periodic Table* (1975), although few were receptive to the book's comic strain.[15]

A similar prejudice exists in the popular view of Franz Kafka's work. His sense of humor is less obvious than that of Levi, but it constitutes an essential element of his vision. Although it has not been ignored by scholars, little has been written about it that has made its way into popular consciousness, and the last thing we usually associate with Kafka is laughter. Yet we know that when Kafka read passages from his manuscripts aloud to friends he would often break out into peals of laughter.

The facts of Kafka's life are well established. He was born in 1883 and raised in a middle-class German and Czech Jewish family in Prague, the eldest of six children, three of whom would later be murdered in the Holocaust. His father was a rather coarse and domineering paterfamilias with whom he had difficult relations all his life. Trained as a lawyer, Kafka spent years in the dreary bureaucracies of the crumbling Austro-Hungarian Empire. Finding the time and appropriate conditions in which to write was a continual challenge. He considered suicide in 1912, the same year that his most famous work, *The Metamorphosis*, came into being. Kafka was drafted for military service in the First World War and he wanted to serve, but his employer arranged a deferment because his work was considered essential government service. In 1917, he was diagnosed with tuberculosis, was put on a pension due to his illness, and spent most of the rest of his life in sanitoriums. He died at the age of forty, leaving only a small collection of works after having burned the majority of his unpublished manuscripts. But, as John Updike wrote, "*The Metamorphosis* alone would assure him a place in world literature."[16]

The novella tells the story of a traveling salesman named Gregor Samsa who wakes up one morning to discover he has been transformed into a gigantic insect. More shocking even than this bizarre fact is that Gregor completely accepts his condition, just as he had always accepted the humiliating conditions of his job. He reflects on his despotic boss, co-workers, and relations with his family, and since the story is told from his point of view, the reader feels in sympathy with him, so much so that at the end when Gregor is dying, we feel a strange, nearly intolerable mixture of pity and horror. Gregor's family has utterly abandoned him and he is a disgusting creature, his carcass reeking with decay, but at this point in the story he is the only character with whom we can possibly identify.

In the opening pages of *The Metamorphosis* Gregor's candid acceptance of his situation has outlandish comic undertones. His brown belly and numerous squirming legs don't upset him in the least; instead, he looks out the window and "the overcast weather completely depressed him."[17] He has trouble getting out of bed because he is lying on his back, which is as hard and heavy as armor, and it's getting late. To make his train, he thinks, he would have to rush, but he "didn't feel especially fresh."[18] Later in the morning, he struggles to turn the key on the lock to his room with his mouth, but "[u]nfortunately, it seemed that he had no real teeth."[19] And, when it comes to escaping his family, who are terrified of him, he discovers that he "had not had any practice at all walking in reverse; it was really very slow going."[20] One can imagine that in hearing Kafka read the narrative aloud, the mounting details of Gregor's physical challenges would take on an almost Chaplinesque humor, as Gregor is defeated at every turn. Unlike the stories Charley Chaplin tells, though, no sentimentality enters into The Metamorphosis to signal the possibility of a happy ending. A sense of defeat is omnipresent because Gregor can no longer be the man, brother, and son he would like to be.

The humor suggests Gregor's independence and resolve "not to be overwhelmed" by his situation.[21] His condition is hopeless but he can witness it with a certain detachment. More might be said about what Walter Benjamin referred to as Kafka's "serenity"[22] and what Thomas Mann may have meant when he called Kafka a "religious humorist,"[23] but I'm interested here in what Kafka's readers might derive from his humor at a basic level. One critic sees a state of mind that "enables the accused to exchange a few jokes with his executioners," but the passages quoted above do not suggest gallows humor.[24] Rather, the humor suggests Gregor's willingness to go on, despite the hopelessness, to the point where we cannot imagine the humor without the hopelessness.

This willingness to go on despite the hopelessness is not very romantic. It doesn't accord with the romantic view of the suffering artist because it implies a detachment from suffering. Kafka's intense personal anguish cannot be doubted. It is evident in his letters and diaries and his novels and stories are generally understood to epitomize the anxiety and alienation of the modern condition. Yet we find mirrored in his style, not romantic agony, but "a conscientious, curiously explicit, objective, clear, and correct" state of mind, as Mann put it.[25] Such a state of mind may not constitute happiness for most people, but it may have given a singular happiness to Kafka.

6

Trollope Today

Novelists go in and out of fashion for complex reasons. In the past fifty years, the same years that saw the decline of D.H. Lawrence's popularity, a remarkable surge of interest in the work of Anthony Trollope has taken place. Trollope is best known for the *Chronicles of Barsetshire,* a series of six novels published between 1855 and 1867 about daily life in the fictitious county of Barset, and another series known as the Palliser novels, which focus on the British political class. Today, biographical and scholarly studies of Trollope abound and TV adaptations of the novels continue to draw large audiences.

So, why Trollope, we may ask, and why now?

As to *why*, most readers no doubt go to the novels for entertainment, which Trollope would have approved. As a professional writer, he wholeheartedly embraced the ancient injunction that art should both delight and instruct, and he produced over forty novels that prove this principle. With varying degrees of success, the novels gracefully disguise his teachings in richly entertaining prose. "It is the test of a novel writer's art that he conceals his snake-in-the-grass," Trollope insisted, "but the reader may be sure it is always there. No man or woman ... with intellect sufficient to produce amusement, can go on from year to year without the desire of teaching."[1]

As to *why now*, perhaps Trollope's fiction is popular today because it teaches readers something they seek to understand, but are uncomfortable acknowledging. No one likes the sight of a snake in the grass. And the knowledge that Trollope's novels obliquely impart is emphatically snake-like in character: cold to the touch and next to impossible to defend against. It's the knowledge that the modern administrative state, in which all of us take part, effectively marginalizes the person of conscience. (It's why today we need laws to protect whistleblowers: in institutional settings, the person of conscience is becoming an endangered species.) Despite the immense advantages of the administrative state, which Trollope consistently acknowledges, this marginalization is unavoidable. When readers close the last novel of the Barset-Palliser series, deserts open up on all sides.

In his life, Trollope was a highly political person. In 1868, he stood as a Liberal candidate in a borough of Yorkshire, spent £400 pounds on his campaign, and finished last in the election. He has much to say about politics in his autobiography and refers to himself as "an advanced Conservative-Liberal."[2] Today the trend is to see Trollope as a liberal or liberal progressive, which paints him as a much more optimistic thinker than he actually was. In a recent essay published in *The Nation*, however, one critic takes a different tact and labels Trollope a radical. He arrives at this conclusion by pointing to a surprising fact. At the end of the six-volume Palliser series, very little has been accomplished. Almost every step forward in liberal reform is followed by a step backward, and the political class as a whole is shown to be fundamentally self-interested and money-driven. This state of affairs prompts the critic to throw up his hands and declare that we "come away from Trollope's constellation of marchionesses and ministers wanting to blow the whole thing up, to sweep the whole system away and start anew. That is the real power of the novels and the reason their vision of politics still feels fresh—because Palliser's world, like ours, is one in which nothing gets done." A profound observation, but one that leads the writer to draw the questionable conclusion that Trollope was "an accidental radical."[3]

The sense in which Trollope may or may not have been "radical" will be taken up later, but it is worth remembering that in any serious work of art nothing is accidental; all of its elements are part of a design. And, in the case of a nineteenth-century realist like Trollope, the design is customized to illuminate social reality, not advance a political position or party. Trollope's decision to portray a state of impasse at the level of parliamentary politics was the result of a long and elaborate study of English life at the atomized level—that is to say, the level of daily communal life in Barset. In the Barset novels, the theme of impasse is present from the first novel of the series, *The Warden* (1855), and is particularly—and acerbically—to be felt in the last two, *The Small House at Allington* (1862–3) and *The Last Chronicle of Barset* (1867). Trollope began the Palliser novels as he was completing the Barset series, almost as if he had been working up to the analysis of high politics in the latter series. He first sought to examine the ways in which the institutions undergirding the political apparatus were operating locally.

By *institutions* I mean the laws, rules, social conventions, and norms that govern the minds and hearts of the characters in Barset and that parliament has the power to reform if enough pressure is brought to bear on its members to do so. Institutions guide the behavior of everyone in Barset, but deviations from institutional norms also take place. Some characters are corrupt and some even engage in crime. Others deviate because they are high-principled; conscience, not convention, guides them. It is in the fate of the high-principled characters that Trollope exposes the curious impasse that will later become the hallmark of parliamentary practice in the Palliser novels. His critique of the administrative state pivots on these highly conscientious characters.

In *The Warden* Trollope introduces this character type, and he will repeat it throughout the Barset series: the honorable person who finds him- or herself in a corrupt system, be it the church, the government, the law, or the social and legal traditions of courtship and marriage. These individuals do not, in the end, succumb to even the most well-meaning efforts of their dearest friends to persuade them to compromise. A clergyman must decide whether or not to give up a generous income managing an almshouse when he no longer feels morally justified in accepting it; a young woman of limited means must decide whether to marry a worthy man she cares for deeply but does not love; an impoverished clergyman unjustly accused of theft must decide if he should take the easy way out by misrepresenting his memory of events. Similar lists of painful but conventional dilemmas may be found in many works of English fiction, but Trollope's narrative of each character's moral struggle is especially riveting because he does not idealize his virtuous characters or demonize their opponents. The high-principled characters always go through a period of moral confusion, although they rarely receive a pat on the back for making the right choice. "The really honest man," Trollope would write in a later novel, "can never say a word to make those who don't know of his honesty believe that it is there."[4]

At stake here is Trollope's pointed awareness of the increasing power of institutions over the daily lives of human beings, and it is this conformity to institutional norms that resonates with the contemporary reader. In our society, the administrative state is much larger than the collected administrative apparatuses of the Victorians. Great Britain's current population of over 66 million and the US population of over 333 million necessitate far more elaborate institutional structures than did the Victorian populace, which rose from roughly 14 million to 32 million between 1831 and 1901. Over this period the diverse institutions of English society gradually synchronized their efforts and the administrative state was born.

It is no wonder, then, that bureaucrats fascinated Trollope, as Adam Gopnick has observed.[5] They would become the unacknowledged legislators of our world.

By focusing on the ordinary person—the well-intentioned but realistically flawed human being—Trollope was able to expose our often conflicted relations with institutions most convincingly. In his world and in our own, a demand is placed on each individual to determine how much of their individuality to give service to laws, rules, social conventions, and norms, and how much to hold back in the name of moral integrity, when institutions are corrupt. Trollope reserves his greatest respect for the characters who imperil themselves because they sincerely accept the rules that order social life and try desperately to maintain their integrity within those rules. He has sympathy for those who go against convention—the unhappily married woman who is led astray or the man who exploits the weaknesses of an institution that is taking advantage of him—but the disaffected and rebellious do not interest him nearly as much as the characters who struggle with their conscience in the face of social disapproval.

The liberal-conservative debate played out at the level of high politics in the Palliser novels is mirrored in the local practices of institutions in Barset. The plot of *The Warden* hinges on a dispute within the Church of England about the management of an almshouse that houses twelve aged men. The charity is supported by the Diocese, which has long provided a comfortable income, including an attractive house and garden, for its kindly warden, Mr. Harding. A dispute arises when a liberal reformer exposes the extent to which the true object of the charity, the humble occupants of the almshouse, are being denied their proper share of the charity's income. Although the Archdeacon and Bishop try to persuade him that he has a legal and moral right to the generous income provided him, Mr. Harding comes to the conclusion that it is wrong for him to accept it and he resigns his office. "He was not so anxious to prove himself right as to be so," writes Trollope in a sentence that encapsulates the unglamorous nature of living according to principle.[6] Mr. Harding moves to rented lodgings in a smaller parish where he lives on a modest income.

At this point, Trollope might have resolved the narrative by suggesting some improvement in the lives of the old men occasioned by Mr. Harding's sacrifice. Instead, when the story ends, the reader learns that the Bishop decides to leave the wardenship vacant. The twelve occupants do not receive an increase in income, and they are now without the benefit of Mr. Harding's loving attention. The liberal reformers have won, insofar as the self-interested practices of church administrators have been nominally changed, but no progress has been made in the care of the poor.

Similar impasses occur at the conclusions of *The Small House in Allington* and *The Last Chronicle of Barset*, but since Trollope's narrator does not generalize about them the way he generalizes about the conduct of individuals, readers tend to overlook them. Trollope's social philosophy is entirely determined by the action of the characters, not by any abstract categories. His narrator does not provide the philosophical distance of a George Eliot narrator, nor does he use terms like "the system" and "systematic" in the manner of Dickens.[7] The great social forces of the period operate unobtrusively through small events, and the characters are unaware that they are in the grip of these forces. All their attention is focused on the particulars of the events engulfing them. Only by standing back and observing the chain of events in their totality can the reader see the full impact of societal constraints on human lives.

The Small House at Allington concerns courtship and marriage traditions. A feckless young man jilts the heroine Lily Dale after he learns that her rich uncle, the patriarch of the family, does not plan to provide a dowry. Although fully aware of her lover's failure of character, Lily remains constant to him. A worthier man, whom she loves as a friend, proposes to her, but she declines, much to the consternation of her friends and family. (When her mother pressures her to accept the offer, Lily asks, "What can a heart be worth if it can be transferred hither and thither as circumstances and convenience and comfort may require?"[8]) Although Lily is shown to be proud and imprudent, she is of course fiercely upholding the Victorian standard of ideal womanhood upon which marriage traditions rely. Yet, when push comes to shove, this is not what the marriage brokers of Barchester really want, and they see Lily as obstinate and unreasonable. Instead of doing what her counterpart, another jilted young woman, does in Jane Austen's *Sense and Sensibility*, Lily refuses to capitulate to the confederacy against her, accept an eligible suitor, and enter the community as a married woman. In her refusal, Lily rejects the idea that woman's highest duty is service to the institution of marriage, and her defiance has the effect of making the community around her slightly nervous. In a brilliantly ambiguous plot twist at the end of the novel, Lily's uncle settles a large sum of money on her to assuage his guilt. Lily is shocked because, as she exclaims, "nobody ever gives girls money like that, so that they can enjoy it."[9] Like everyone else in the community, her uncle does not want to acknowledge that Lily is a victim of society's marriage norms, and he therefore gives her something like legal compensation for the failure of the social system. This is the "snake-in-the-grass" of *The Small House at Allington.*

"Of all novelists in any country," wrote W.H. Auden, "Trollope best understands the role of money."[10] This is particularly true of *The Last Chronicle of Barset,* in which the plot revolves around the suffering of Josiah Crawley, an impoverished parson unfairly accused of theft. Crawley is an intellectually gifted and deeply spiritual man who suffers under a brutal system of patronage that leaves him unable to adequately support his family. When charged with the crime, Crawley is too proud to defend himself effectively and, nearly broken by poverty, he begins to doubt his own memory of events surrounding the alleged theft. Crawley is eventually exonerated but the seriousness of the harm done to him is not something the community wishes to acknowledge.

Trollope resolves Crawley's situation by means of a subplot. It happens that the son of the wealthy Archdeacon is in love with Crawley's beautiful and learned daughter Grace. The Archdeacon opposes the marriage because of Grace's poverty, but, pressured by his wife, he finally agrees to it. And, given that he does not want déclassé relatives in the family, the Archdeacon decides to raise Crawley's status by offering him a respectable and lucrative post.

In the hands of a different novelist this resolution might have been presented simply as the proverbial happy ending, but Trollope chose to shine too strong a light on the Archdeacon's smarminess in his concluding interview with Crawley. Readers are glad that Crawley has been spared prison and that he and his family will be better off, but they also register the church's adaptability and talent for consolidating its power.

In Trollope's world, institutions maintain the status quo by *appearing* to implement positive changes and reforms.[11] The telos of all the activity in a Trollope novel, with its endlessly intricate plot, is the consolidation of institutional authority. Ultimately Trollope does not allow the high principled characters to effect social change or even to impact other characters in the profound way virtuous characters often do in Austen and Dickens; these characters stand for individual conscience alone. When Mr. Harding decides to renounce his beloved post, he does so on the basis of "an inward and an unguided conviction of my own."[12]

Like many other nineteenth-century writers conscious of events that took place in France in 1789, Trollope believed in the importance of stability, and to him that meant the stability of institutions and of the growing middle class. He appears to make his upright characters work hard to give that stability meaning. What is really suggested in the novels, however, is not meaningful stability but impasse. The resolutions of these novels point to the emergence of the administrative state of mind that dominates the political class of the Palliser novels. The glacial rate of progress is the inevitable consequence of a functioning bureaucracy. And while at first glance a condition of impasse may seem to work against the sacrificing of individuals—Mr. Harding, Lily Dale, and Crawley are all relatively contented at the end of their stories—profound sacrifices have taken place. The virtuous individual is seen in his or her isolation. In a world made up of self-interested, compromised people, the individual who is not self-interested is barely tolerated.

Trollope was not a "radical," then, in that he did not call for the systematic overhauling of institutions. However fierce his disgust over the abuses of the Established Church and the aristocracy, his novels exhibit a fondness for their traditions. His faith in community, to the extent that it exists, is embodied in those rare individuals whose singular honesty quietly upholds the doctrines informing the ancient institutions that have been overrun by power-seekers and bureaucrats. Institutions remain, but efforts to reform them in any meaningful way end in impasse. As a man, Trollope sincerely believed in liberal reform, but as a novelist he had a duty to demonstrate the truth: the administrative state encourages conformity and works to dull the conscience of all but a few individuals in any given locale. The person of conscience is *systematically* marginalized. To the extent that Trollope's increasingly administered society looks forward to our own, this should be a warning to us. And yet it is a warning that contemporary critics of Trollope often ignore. In their eagerness to label him a conservative, liberal, or radical—he has been called all three—they are missing the most relevant piece of political wisdom he has to offer us.

PART THREE

CREEDLESS RELIGION AND UNBRIDLED PHILOSOPHICAL SPECULATION

7

Self-Help Literature and the Vanishing Legacy of Thomas Carlyle

Anyone who has frequented big retail bookstores in recent years may have noticed the steady increase of literature devoted to self-help. Oddly, while this trend would seem to point to a growing appreciation of the virtues of self-sufficiency, it may also be having the opposite effect. Most self-help books of today appear to be based on a fundamental contradiction. They propose to educate readers in self-reliance by urging them to rely on the author's advice. Perhaps this is why the majority of self-help customers today are "repeat customers" who continue to buy the literature even when it has not helped them.[1] Self-help books are often a symptom of the disease they purport to cure—but what is the disease?

The Scottish philosopher Thomas Carlyle had an answer to this question. In 1834, he published a philosophical novel in which the concept of self-help plays a pivotal role. Of course, the term *self-help* did not mean to him what it does to us today. To Carlyle, it probably would have called to mind the Stoic philosophers of the ancient world, like Epictetus and Marcus Aurelius, who wrote prescriptive works of lasting literary value. But Carlyle would also have noticed the burgeoning self-improvement movement in the England of his day. Spawned by popular commercial publications such as George Combe's *The Constitution of Man* (1828) and Samuel Smiles's *Self-Help* (1859), this movement spread to other countries and had considerable impact over time. Today the self-improvement market in the United States alone includes books, audio cassettes, personal coaching services, software programs, and more, and has an estimated worth of over 13 billion dollars. When Carlyle made the concept of self-help vital to his narrative of self-fashioning, he was not seeking to ally himself with any new initiative or group of people. But it is no coincidence that he was composing this work when the self-help movement was gaining ground.

Why did the self-improvement movement arise in Victorian England? The most common explanation is that it answered the needs of industrial capitalism.[2] England was the first country in the world to become industrialized, and therefore the first to produce an ideology of personal self-discipline that would serve the competitive new economy. Smiles's book championed the practical virtues of self-help, industry, and perseverance, and was an instant success. Before Queen Victoria died in 1901 the book had been translated into over a dozen languages and was particularly successful in America.

Alongside the immense changes wrought by industrialization to people's work lives, however, was a more inward and possibly more catastrophic change: the widespread decline in religious faith, a consequence largely of the impact of scientific discoveries that undermined confidence in the literal truth of the Bible. Although early self-help literature has a practical focus, it places great importance on *believing in oneself*, a goal that has persisted to the present. What choice was there, once belief in something transcendent had disappeared?

One account of personal crisis published in the 1830s describes a young man who, having lost his conventional religious faith, is driven to despair. Since his belief in himself had hinged on belief in a Christian God, he could find no solace in the rationalistic theology known as Deism, according to which God exists but does not intervene in human life or interact with humankind. Such an "absentee God, sitting idle ... at the outside of his Universe" gave the young man no "life-warmth,"[3] no deep personal knowledge that he was valued. In the absence of such "life-warmth," the universe becomes a giant apparatus, a "huge, dead, immeasurable Steam-engine, rolling on, in its dead indifference, to grind me limb from limb."[4]

The young man's name is Diogenes *Teufelsdröckh*—a comically bizarre name I will discuss shortly—and he is a fictitious character in the philosophical narrative alluded to above: Carlyle's *Sartor Resartus*, a work that, fifty years ago, was a standard part of any college English curriculum.[5] Carlyle based his story on the spiritual crisis he himself underwent as a poor and lonely young man trying to make his way in Scotland in the early nineteenth century. Like Carlyle's own experience of unrelenting misery, Diogenes' crisis is brought on by the loss of religious faith, and is resolved without the aid of doctrine. He becomes, in effect, his own therapist, solving his problems inwardly.

An ego made whole without recourse to formal religion is likewise the goal of much psychotherapy in secular society. It's what contemporary self-help books characteristically aim for and one reason Carlyle's story is relevant to the present. *Sartor Resartus* had an immense impact on English and American readers throughout the nineteenth century but, strangely enough, it may be even more useful to readers today. Teaching by example, *Sartor Resartus* tells the story of how one individual acquires "for himself the highest of all possessions, that of Self-help."[6]

How does Diogenes come to believe in himself? How does he make himself whole? In his wretchedness he is constantly contemplating suicide, but a certain "aftershine" of Christianity, as he puts it, holds him back, together with the reassuring knowledge that death will not forsake him. ("Destiny itself could not doom me not to die," he thinks.) Living without hope, he has no fear of death; in fact, he has no "definite" fears at all, yet he confesses to living in a continual, "indefinite" state of apprehension, a whining, cowering, whimpering fear of "I knew not what."[7]

One day, while toiling along a filthy street in Paris in the dog days of summer, he finally dares to ask himself what he is so afraid of. What is the worst that can happen to him, the "sum-total of the worst" that lies before him?[8] Out of the blue, a thought comes to him—Have I not a "heart"? that is to say, courage?—and he shakes off his fears. "Let it come, then; I will meet it and defy it!" he proclaims, his "whole Me" standing up to record its protest. Such a protest is "the most important transaction in Life … [from] a *psychological* point of view," writes Carlyle [my italics], because at this moment Diogenes fully embraces self-help, "the highest of all possessions."[9] His "I" and his "Me" come together at last.

Heart or courage is not the same as fearlessness, as the Cowardly Lion famously learns in *The Wizard of Oz*; it's the ability to face one's fears. Until he realizes this, the poor Lion is a hopeless neurotic. "I even scare myself," he whimpers in the film, "Look at the circles under my eyes, I haven't slept in weeks!"[10] In his cowering state, the Lion cannot distinguish among his fears, but once he has found his courage, he is able to choose the right course of action. In Aristotelian ethics, courage is the cardinal virtue that enables us to moderate our fears and thereby choose good. The root of the word courage is *cor*—the Latin word for heart. (*Cor* is cognate with Old English *heorte*, Greek *kardia*, and possibly Latin *crēdere*, to believe.) Given the word's grounding in the wellspring of feeling, it's not surprising that in works of literature concerned with questions of courage and cowardice, like Joseph Conrad's *Lord Jim*, the protagonist who puts these questions to the test remains an enigma.

In an observation that would have pleased Carlyle, Conrad writes of "how incomprehensible, wavering, and misty" are the souls of human beings.[11] It is because Diogenes is a mystery *to himself* that he needs courage, and his newly found faith in himself is the basis of the creedless religion he embraces. According to Carlyle, "the fearful Unbelief" in God afflicting his fellow Victorians is "unbelief in yourself."[12]

The word *courage* is rarely mentioned in many self-help books today. It's possible that this is the single most revealing fact about them. In scanning entries under the letter C in the index of a recent bestseller, for example, I found rational concepts like *counsel* and *coping style*, but not *courage*. "Coping style" appears in the text as #5 on a checklist of seven goals for achieving "wellness." According to the author, it is an "adaptive" method of confronting and "appraising [problems] without excessive rumination, unhealthy emotional reactions, or avoidance behavior."[13] In *Sartor Resartus*, excessive rumination and unhealthy emotional reactions take up years of Diogenes's life. These forms of behavior are not overcome by an adaptive method of rational appraisal but by summoning the courage to defy them inwardly.

Carlyle was a philosopher and therefore perhaps naturally given to "excessive rumination," but in the crucial passage quoted above, he elevates Heart over Head. So did John Stuart Mill, Carlyle's most rationalistic contemporary and one of his greatest admirers, when he underwent a spiritual crisis comparable to that of Carlyle. Dwelling on an inspired act of courage on the part of a character in a book he was reading, Mill writes: "A vivid conception of the scene and its feelings came over me, and I was moved to tears … I was no longer hopeless: I was not a stock or a stone. I had still, it seemed, some of the material out of which all worth of character [is] made."[14] Mill appropriates the "feeling" of courage from an example in a book.

It doesn't matter that the act of courage being described is performed by a character in a story Mill is reading, or that the life circumstances of the character are completely different from his own. What matters is that the representation of courage is context-specific, put forth not in a general maxim but evoked in the particulars of lived experience. Similarly, neither Carlyle nor Mill universalizes their own crises by laying claim to a fixed set of principles or moral directives to be understood rationally, as in much self-help literature. Instead, they offer a dynamic model that can be grasped as a standard and therefore serve as inspiration.

The typical self-help book of today lacks the sense of urgency that necessitates a transformative response, such as a work of imaginative literature can elicit. And this is not because self-help writers are untalented. Simply by virtue of their undemanding style, they come across as condescending. The main ideas on how to achieve happiness—the pre-eminent goal of most self-help books—are usually displayed on the book jacket.[15] The author then fleshes them out, chapter after chapter, with personal anecdotes and the occasional scientific study. The author assures us that deep personal change is just around the corner. But as we read on, the number of random tasks assigned to prepare us for our transformation belies this claim. Keep a journal, take up yoga, learn to meditate, and build a support group, the author advises. In this type of self-help book, readers are rarely urged to confront their problems directly.[16] If they could do that, they probably would not be buying self-help books, which the author well knows.

The idea of the self informing much self-help literature tends to be rather bland and rose-colored. In a surprising number of self-help books, a pollyannish view of human nature is allied with a facile Buddhism. Even when the author is a recognized authority on Buddhism, the popularization of religious ideas tends to result in a wilderness of platitudes and promises.[17] If readers adopt such and such practices, the author asserts, they will achieve happiness. This may turn out to be true, but in making the adoption of Buddhist practices sound simple and easily attainable, self-help authors inadvertently mislead their readers. Serene faith in the essential goodness of human nature seems to be both a requirement and a goal of self-help in books of this type.

Given Carlyle's roots in Scottish Calvinism, not to mention his sardonic sense of humor, he probably would have viewed the premise of untroubled faith in human nature with skepticism, if not scorn. His understanding of human character is comically embedded in the meaning of his hero's name—God-born Devil's Dung. To Carlyle, we are inwardly drawn in opposite directions. Possessed of both good and evil impulses, each of us is a walking contradiction and ultimately a mystery. According to his way of thinking, then, the disease that self-help books propose to cure is that of being human. The only solution to this unhappy and often ridiculous condition is heroic struggle on the part of the self to master its own waywardness.

Accordingly, Diogenes does not enter into a state of unclouded happiness after his bold act of defiance. True to the discovery of his own courage, he goes on to explore and ultimately reject the Happiness Ideal, insisting that it is not in his nature to be happy. "Man's Unhappiness, as I construe, comes of his Greatness; it is because there is an Infinite in him, which with all his cunning he cannot quite bury under the Finite."[18] Do without happiness, Diogenes tells himself. Find the work in life you were meant to do and do it with all your might, "for the Night cometh, wherein no man can work."[19] Many Americans are of course unwilling to relinquish happiness as an ideal, given that our declarations of independence—both personal and national—are traditionally bound up with the pursuit of happiness. But in *Sartor Resartus*, the entire question of happiness looks very different to Diogenes once he has summoned the courage to be. He is now able to turn outward toward the world and embrace many possibilities, including that of happiness.

Born in 1795, Carlyle began his career as a political and philosophical radical whose works would greatly impact the rise of socialist thought.

But later in his life—he died in 1881—he published vehemently anti-democratic and racist essays that partially account for his current unpopularity among academics.[20] When I was an undergraduate English major in the late 1960s, Carlyle's importance to the study of Victorian literature was unquestioned, not only because of the power and originality of his prose but because of the impact of his thought on later writers, including continental and American writers.[21] Our Victorian prose anthology opened with a 257-page selection of Carlyle's writings, a quarter of which was taken from *Sartor Resartus*.[22] The standard anthology of Victorian literature today (Volume E of the *Norton Anthology of English Literature*) contains merely twenty-five pages of Carlyle selections.[23] *Sartor Resartus* is not among them, even though it is generally recognized to be one of Carlyle's masterpieces. Mention is made of *Sartor* in a commentary on Carlyle's life and career that describes it as a work of philosophy. No student using the anthology could ever guess that the work contains a passionate narrative of the turning point in a man's life.

The decision to marginalize Carlyle in this way should not be seen in exclusively political terms if only because we can find instances of racist, imperialist, or reactionary sentiment in writers who have maintained their importance on the Victorian syllabus. Charlotte Brontë, Mill, and Dickens are three examples.[24] Carlyle expressed his views in more offensive language than did these writers, but his views were not in themselves unusual for the period.

It would seem to be Carlyle's renegade religiosity and his famously "volcanic," uninhibited style—in short, his literary-philosophical radicalism—that repel contemporary scholars. Two such scholars, editors of an influential anthology of Victorian literature that eliminates selections from Carlyle's major works, complain that beneath his "moral vehemence … one looks in vain for any anchorage more substantial than awed reverence before the … spirit of the age."[25] Yet the experience of reading an "unanchored" style, in which the author habitually creates neologisms and untoward metaphors, is itself the message. Coming up with his own language is essential to the announced intention of *Sartor*: the repudiation of established institutions, including the language that institutions have enshrined. Writers have always understood this; Oscar Wilde knew sections of Carlyle's works by heart and would recite them at length to friends. Today's academics tend to characterize this style as merely idiosyncratic and extravagant, as if it were so much rodomontade, rather than the consciously unpredictable, wildly allusive music that Wilde and many others have found it to be.

"We speak of the Volume of Nature: and truly a Volume it is," writes Carlyle in a typically multivalent sentence of *Sartor* composed in anapestic meter.[26] To Carlyle, the legible volume of nature was immense indeed; to read and study it, polymath that he was, he drew on astronomy, mathematics, geology, history, and law in addition to theology, philosophy, and literature. Teaching such allusive prose to today's students is admittedly difficult, but I have found that they appreciate Carlyle's lack of condescension. His writing possesses nothing of what Nietzsche refers to as the "insulting clarity" of prose that carefully adapts itself to the presumed lesser knowledge of the reader.[27]

In a recent essay in the *London Review of Books* Stefan Collini remarks on the difficulty readers may have in understanding why so many young people of the 1830s and 1840s found Carlyle "an inspiringly positive moral guide."[28] This is because college students no longer read *Sartor Resartus*. When Carlyle wrote *Sartor*, he was attempting to establish himself as an author, but in narrating his journey from the "The Everlasting No" to the "The Everlasting Yea" he earned the title of moral teacher. He strengthened his authority to assume this mantle in later works like *Past and Present*. But without giving his readers a narrative of his own passionate struggle to affirm the worth of his existence, he would not have won the following he did. Readers embrace a moral teacher when they recognize an authentic life, and *Sartor Resartus* is part of a tradition of autobiography that models the life worth living. The tradition of autobiography as philosophical argument begins in Western literature with the life of Socrates as narrated by Plato. The Victorians, who were deeply engaged with ancient Greek literature, embraced this tradition, producing autobiographies of lasting importance like those of Carlyle, Mill, John Henry Newman, and Oscar Wilde. To drop *Sartor Resartus* from this list is to eliminate the work that influenced all the later exemplars. As George Eliot once suggested, if all of Carlyle's books were burnt, "it would only be like cutting down an oak after its acorns have sown a forest."[29]

Returning *Sartor Resartus* to the literary syllabus will also ensure that at least some readers develop a sense of what self-help actually looks and feels like. College students in particular would benefit from such illumination, but only a demanding prose can provide it. The struggle to believe in oneself is no doubt a laborious process, but it can open possibilities. When Diogenes finally summons his courage and ceases to "eat his own heart," he does not find the peace he desires. He instead turns restlessly outward toward the many-colored world, toward the "Not-me," in search of "wholesomer food."[30]

8

"My Life, My *Real* Life"

In 1955, James Baldwin published the now famous *Notes of a Native Son*, a collection of autobiographical essays written in his twenties. In the title essay he vividly describes growing up in Harlem as the oldest of nine children; his troubled relationship with his preacher father; his decision to preach himself; his final break with the church at the age of seventeen; and his initial experiences with Jim Crow segregation and Black resistance. The essay ends with his father's funeral, which took place on his nineteenth birthday and on the same day as the Harlem riot of 1943. His mother could not attend because she was in the hospital recovering from the birth of her ninth child.

Baldwin is at a pivotal moment in his life. Filled with anger against his father and outrage at the injustices to which he is daily witness, he is increasingly aware that "my life, my *real* life, was in danger, and not from anything other people might do but from the hatred I carried in my heart."[1] He knows he must make a choice, and on the way to his father's burial he makes it: "It was necessary to hold on to the things that mattered. The dead man mattered, the new life mattered; Blackness and whiteness did not matter; to believe that they did was to acquiesce in one's own destruction. Hatred, which could destroy so much, never failed to destroy the man who hated and this was an immutable law."[2] He pledges to fight injustices with all his strength, but this fight begins "in the heart and it now had been laid to my charge to keep my own heart free of hatred and despair."[3]

Notes of a Native Son is the work to which most readers turn to understand Baldwin's life, even though he published a more mature, and no less essential, memoir when he was fifty-two.[4] The later collection of essays, *The Devil Finds Work*, is an irreplaceable addendum to the first. For here it's not only what Baldwin suffered that matters; it's how he came to bear his suffering and view it over time, and how he managed to keep his pledge.

In celebration of the one-hundredth anniversary of Baldwin's birth in 1924, the *New York Times* published several appreciations of his work, including Robert Jones Jr.'s "The Essential James Baldwin." Jones names *The Devil Finds Work* as Baldwin's "most underrated book."[5] Not surprisingly, when the book first appeared, it struck some reviewers as eclectic to a fault.[6] It opens with autobiography and then shifts to film criticism, and the ten films discussed are not in chronological order. But, like any work of art, the book has its own logic, one that most certainly was intentional on Baldwin's part. Part 1 recounts his moral and aesthetic education; Part 2, the moral and aesthetic education of his country in the temple of popular art. Part 3, a masterpiece of intellectual scaffolding, goes from Baldwin's brief stint as screenwriter for *The Autobiography of Malcolm X*, his interpretation of that film and two others (about Che Guevara and Billie Holiday) to a profound cultural analysis of the 1973 film *The Exorcist* in the context of Baldwin's own experience and understanding of religion. At the exact center of *The Devil Finds Work*, in the middle of a seemingly random paragraph in Part 2, Baldwin lights on the main theme of the work: "in order for a person to bear his life, he needs a valid re-creation of that life."[7]

Whether one likes the style of this work may depend on whether one is responsive to another art form: modern jazz. In a symposium of authors in 1962, Baldwin said this about his style: "I really do not, at the very bottom of my own mind, compare myself to other writers. I think I really helplessly model myself on jazz musicians and try to write the way they sound . . . . I am aiming at what Henry James called 'perception at the pitch of passion.'"[8] The velocity of Baldwin's prose, its arresting turns, retreats, and sudden leaps forward, its melancholy and humor, and its overall improvisational structure, expressiveness, and sense of immediacy—all mimic the sound variations of modern jazz. (Baldwin particularly admired Miles Davis.) Even in the most analytical sections of *The Devil Finds Work*, one must *hear* Baldwin to grasp his meaning.

Reflecting on his earliest memories from the distance of four decades, Baldwin adopts a ruminative rhythm, often repeating the same words, as if he is talking to himself: "I knew that I was poor, and knew that I was black, but did not yet know what being black really meant, what it meant, that is, in the history of my country, and in my own history."[9] In Part 1 of *The Devil Finds Work* he demonstrates how his early experience of film and theater lights his path to an understanding of what being Black meant. This education is by no means simple. The films he saw were primarily about white people—when Black actors like Stepin Fetchit were featured, young Baldwin loathed them—and he is so overpowered by the first play he sees that he joins a Pentecostal church and stops attending films and plays altogether for three years.

If we compare Baldwin's aesthetic education to that of the white authors he read in his youth—say, Charles Dickens—the complicated, indirect nature of his development becomes clear. As a boy, Dickens delighted in eighteenth-century novels and the Arabian tales, a delight that he recreates in his autobiographical novel *David Copperfield*. "They kept alive my fancy, and my hope of something beyond that place in time," says David. So robust is David's identification with the heroes of the novels that he impersonated them: "I have been Tom Jones … for a week together."[10] Baldwin's path to self-affirmation was more treacherous. It was less a matter of direct identification with characters than a search for meaning.

The Devil Finds Work begins with what must be one of the most ambiguous opening images of any autobiography in English: "Joan Crawford's straight, narrow, and lonely back. We are following her through the corridors of a moving train. She is looking for someone, or she is trying to escape from someone."[11] The reference is to Crawford's performance in the 1931 film *Dance, Fools, Dance*, which Baldwin saw at around the age of seven. He does not remember the film, only the image.

> … I was aware that Joan Crawford was a white lady. Yet, I remember being sent to the store sometime later, and a colored woman, who, to me, looked like Joan Crawford, was buying something. She was

> so incredibly beautiful—she seemed to be wearing the sunlight, rearranging it around her from time to time, with a movement of one hand, with a movement of her head, and with her smile—that, when she paid the man and started out of the store, I started out behind her. The storekeeper, who knew me, and others in the store who knew my mother's little boy (and who also knew my Miss Crawford!) laughed and called me back. Miss Crawford also laughed and looked down at me with so beautiful a smile that I was not even embarrassed. Which was rare for me.[12]

The image of Crawford introduced the little boy to an ideal of beauty that he then transferred across races. In the above passage, Crawford's screen image is conflated with the black woman in the store to the point where the latter and "Miss Crawford" become one. Thus, one page later, when a white teacher who will shepherd his intellectual growth enters his "terrifying life," she is described as "beautiful."[13] Because of Miss Miller, "I never really managed to hate white people."[14] But since she "was not at all like the cops who had already beaten me up [and] she was not like the landlords who called me nigger," the boy is completely baffled.

The "unfathomable question" for the child then became:

> what, under heaven, or beneath the sea, or in the catacombs of hell, could cause any people to act as white people acted? From Miss Miller, therefore, I began to suspect that *white people did not act as they did because they were white, but for some other reason*, and I began to try to locate and understand the reason. She, too, anyway, was treated like a nigger, especially by the cops, and she had no love for landlords (my italics).[15]

Just as *beauty* emerges in the boy's consciousness as an ideal, *virtue* emerges as an ideal, independent of the material facts of race. How else is an artist born out of a life as "terrifying" as that of Baldwin, if not by constructing ideals, as fragile as such ideals inevitably are?

Notes of a Native Son gives us the dramatic record of his terror, whereas *The Devil Finds Work* is a sober recollection of how he coped with it inwardly: the beginnings of a lifelong struggle against fear and hatred. The paragraph following immediately upon the above-quoted passage introduces the first, almost comic challenge in this struggle: "My father said, during all the years I lived with him, that I was the ugliest boy he had ever seen, and I had absolutely no reason to doubt him."[16] Beauty. Then ugliness—his own ugliness.

The boy's contemplation of his ugliness and the fact of his Blackness are woven into discussions of the films and novels that engage him in these years: *20,000 Years in Sing-Sing* with Bette Davis (who has Baldwin's same "pop-eyes" and who "moved just like a nigger"); Harriet Beecher Stowe's *Uncle Tom's Cabin* (the novel) and Dickens' *A Tale of Two Cities* (the novel and the 1935 film adaptation); Fyodor Dostoevsky's *Crime and Punishment* (the novel); *You Only Live Once* and *Fury* (early films directed by Fritz Lang); and others. In contemplating these narratives the boy seeks to understand "where blacks fit," which is to say, where *he* fit.[17] He is "not misled … by the surface of these novels ….I did not believe in any of these people so much as I believed in their situation, which I suspected, dreadfully, to have something to do with my own."[18] In Blanche Yurka's performance of Madame Defarge in the film *A Tale of Two Cities* "I recognized that unrelenting hatred, for it was all up and down my streeets, and in my father's face and voice."[19] The film also introduces him to the idea of revolution.

Then Miss Miller takes him to see his first play, the Orson Wells production of *Macbeth* with an all-Black cast, at the Lafayette Theater in Harlem. "I am about twelve or thirteen," writes Baldwin. "I can be fairly certain about all this, because my life changed so violently when I entered the church, and I entered the church around the time of fourteen. When I entered the church, I ceased going to the theater."[20]

The incipient bodily consciousness of early adolescence is emotionally fraught for many people, but for a young boy who saw himself as ugly, who was Black living in a racist society, and who was beginning to discover his homosexuality, it presented an overpowering challenge. Baldwin's father viewed his son's literary and cinematic interests as a threat to his son's salvation; he deeply distrusted Miss Miller's influence, and, as a preacher, he would have disapproved of homosexuality. The church gave Baldwin a disguise for self-hatred, as he would later realize. But what was it about seeing *Macbeth* on stage that precipitated this crisis of renunciation?

As in the case of the Joan Crawford film, Baldwin's receptivity to works of art lies at the center of his development. In *Macbeth*, the people he is watching on the stage "were black, like me. Nothing that I had seen before prepared me for this."[21] Whereas the distance between a movie audience and the screen image is "a paradoxical absolute, masquerading as intimacy" that allows the viewer to surrender to the corroboration of his fantasies, the tension in a theater possesses a different sort of immediacy.[22]

> One is not in the presence of shadows, but responding to one's flesh and blood. In the theater, we are re-creating each other ....Nor, in the present instance, is the term "one's flesh and blood" meant to

> refer, merely, to the spectacle of a black boy seeing, for the first time in his life, living black actors on a living stage: we are *all* each other's flesh and blood.[23]

The fact that he is seeing bodies on the stage is as crucial as the fact that they are Black bodies. And the whole experience is overwhelming: "Flesh and blood had proved to be too much for flesh and blood." The young teenager suddenly finds himself on the floor of the Pentacostal church "crying holy unto the Lord."[24]

Three years pass as Baldwin enters on a vocation as preacher before a friend confronts him with his hypocrisy. Because he entered the church less to save his soul than to escape it, the friend pleads with him to reconsider his vocation, arguing that staying in the church "was unutterably far beneath me, and too despicable a cowardice for him to support in any friend of his."[25] The friend buys tickets to a matinee performance of *Native Son*, directed by Orson Wells, at the St. James Theater, and says he will be waiting for Baldwin to meet him at 2 p.m. the following Sunday.

In *The Fire Next Time*, published over a decade before *The Devil Finds Work*, Baldwin had already recounted what life had been like in the church. It offered him excitement, music, and drama, but it also exposed him to a hypocrisy among the ministers that was "deeper, deadlier, and more subtle" than any hypocrisy exposed in the film *Elmer Gantry*. He began to feel he was committing a crime when he preached to the children in Harlem "to reconcile themselves with their misery on earth in order the gain the crown of eternal life."

> Were only Negroes to gain this crown? Was Heaven, then, to be merely another ghetto? Perhaps I might have been able to reconcile

> myself even to this if I had been able to believe that there was any loving-kindness to be found in the haven I represented. But I had been in the pulpit too long and I had seen too many monstrous things. I don't refer merely to the glaring fact that the minister eventually acquires houses and Cadillacs while the faithful continue to scrub floors and drop their dimes and quarters and dollars into the plate. I really mean that there was no love in the church. It was a mask for hatred and self-hatred and despair.[26]

On the Sunday following his conversation with his friend, Baldwin left the church forever.

He attends the matinee of *Native Son* and, as in the *Macbeth* performance, Baldwin is overwhelmed by the bodily presence of actors. Canada Lee's presence in the role of Bigger Thomas, "gave me the right to live. He was not at the mercy of my imagination, as he would have been, on the screen: he was on the stage, in flesh and blood, and I was, therefore, at the mercy of *his* imagination."[27] Whereas the camera "sees what you want it to see," stage actors have the potential to confront, rather than confirm, our illusions. "The language of the camera is the language of our dreams."[28] It follows, then, that the camera has the power to give expression to our collective fantasies.

In Part 2 Baldwin analyzes ten popular movies, all of which either include Black actors or engage questions of race indirectly. The discussion ranges over a period of fifty-two years, from *The Birth of a Nation* (1915) to *In the Heat of the Night* (1967). Some of Baldwin's observations will seem obvious to us today unless we bear in mind his central premise: that "all men are brothers."[29]

In the Heat of the Night imagines itself about brotherhood, for example, but the friendship that develops between a southern white sheriff and a northern Black investigator conceals the ruinous implication of the plot: "The life of Virgil Tibbs (Sidney Poitier) is endangered precisely to the extent that we are concerned about the salvation of the Sheriff's soul."[30] The sheriff (Rod Steigger) and other white townspeople in the film "can be considered moving and pathetic only if one has the luxury of the assurance that one will never be at their mercy."[31] In discussing *The Defiant Ones,* Baldwin again shows how a film can assuage a white audience's guilt by satisfying its need to be saved: "Liberal white audiences applauded when Sydney [Poitier], at the end of the film, jumped off the train in order not to abandon his white buddy," giving up his own hope for freedom. "The Harlem audience was outraged, and yelled *Get back on the train, you fool!*" What better forgiveness than to be saved by the one you have injured?

Certain rules restricting the emergence of brotherhood are observed in almost all the films. "A black man and white man can come together only in the absence of women" (*The Defiant Ones*).[32] The inclusion of the figure of the loyal Black maid (loyal to her white employer) appears to be "absolutely obligatory" in any number of films about race, from *Birth of a Nation* to *Gone With the Wind* and *Guess Who's Coming to Dinner?*[33] As concerns the latter liberal icon, we can conclude that a Black man has the right to marry a white woman if he is a world-famous doctor, if he has shown that he can restrain himself sexually, and if he refuses to marry her without her parents' permission. It helps, too, if the interacial couple leaves town when dinner is over and plans to live abroad.[34]

As suggested at the outset of this essay, the main theme of *The Devil Finds Work*—that "in order for a person to bear his life, he needs a valid re-creation of that life"—is stated at the center of Part 2. Here Baldwin writes as a Black man in search of a valid cinematic re-creation of Black existence, using movies "as catalysts for an extensive study of the American psyche, his own life, and the sociopolitical climate in America." Baldwin's authorized biographer David Leeming is one of the few commentators fully to appreciate how deeply *The Devil Finds Work* reaches into "the sacrosanct classics of the 'temple' and the politically correct films of the post-civil rights period" in order to educate both Black and white readers in the pervasiveness of racism.[35]

In the act of analyzing our collective fantasies as epitomized by Hollywood, Baldwin does not find the valid re-creations of life that he wants. American popular culture comes up short, because American culture comes up short. But he puts on record his analyses of some of the most popular films ever made. A comparable study of the American psyche in a work of cultural criticism that appeared in the same period is Michael Wood's *America in the Movies*, which shares some of Baldwin's main assumptions. Wood draws on the French Marxist philosopher Louis Althusser to suggest that the influence of the movies lies in "the pictures of probability that people have, in their sense of the world's workings, in their ideologies." Ideology has little to do with conscious thought. It imposes itself on us by means of the "structures of moral and mental life in America" of which we are barely aware. Ideology—like the myth that "nice guys finish last" (Wood) or the belief that Black men pose a sexual threat to white women (Baldwin)—exists in both society and in film. "Popular movies take up wishes, dreads, and preoccupations that are loosely (and sometimes not so loosely) scattered about ordinary life, and give them a lodging in fiction, allow them a quick, masked passage across our consciousness," writes Wood.[36] The key word here is *masked*. The serious problems that popular films address are located in the subtext, but they can never be cured because they are never confronted. Popular films "permit us to look without looking at things we can neither face fully nor entirely disavow."[37]

By the end of Part 2 of *The Devil Finds Work*, the sociology of films opens out into the sociology of American life, as Baldwin tells the story of his encounter with the FBI in 1945. The story is preceded by his analysis of a McCarthyite film called *My Son, John* (1952) that celebrates the FBI. Baldwin's personal experience of interrogation and surveillance returns the reader to political reality, and he now moves naturally to Part 3, which begins with discussions of "real people"—Malcolm X, Che Guevara, and Billie Holiday—and how Hollywood whitewashes their stories. What keeps this particular discussion from seeming obvious is the narrative beginning Part 3 in which Baldwin tells of his own experience in Hollywood when he accepted an invitation to write the screenplay for *The Autobiography of Malcom X*.

The studio assigned Baldwin a "technical" expert whose job was to collaborate with him in translating his ideas into cinematic language. When Baldwin notices that "all meaning was being siphoned out of [his scenes]," he intercepts an inter-office memo stipulating that "the writer (me) should be advised that the tragedy of Malcolm's life was that he had been mistreated, early, by some whites, and betrayed (later) by *many* blacks: emphasis in the original. The writer was also to avoid suggesting that Malcolm's trip to Mecca could have had any political implications or repercussions."[38] Baldwin wants us to see how skillfully a potentially revolutionary film is defanged before it reaches the consumer. Such films invite us superficially to remember figures like Malcolm X, Che, and Billie Holiday so as really to forget them. One is reminded of the pious and reassuring eulogies delivered at memorial services.

In the final pages of *The Devil Finds Work*, Baldwin takes up the film *The Exorcist,* which he first saw with a friend in Hollywood and then saw again, alone. "I tried to be absolutely open to it, suspending judgment as totally as I could. For, after all, if I had once claimed to be 'filled' with the Holy Ghost, and had once really believed, after all, that the Holy Ghost spoke through me, I could not, out of hand, arbitrarily sneer at the notion of demonic possession."[39] Thus, Baldwin begins his discussion of *The Exorcist* by recalling his conversion experience at the age of fourteen.

Baldwin takes for granted our awareness that he left the church long ago, as evident from Part 1 and from his scathing description of the church in *The Fire Next Time.* Nevertheless, the vague assumption persists, even among several of his biographers, that he never really freed himself from the church.[40] No doubt Baldwin learned some of his "verbal flamboyance" from his early years preaching, but once he had broken with the church, his allusions to an unseen reality—"my *real* life"—suggest an engagement with creedless religion, not church nostalgia.[41] The idea of religiosity seems to baffle many people, as if the only legitimate religious feeling available to human beings is to be found in collective worship, an idea that Baldwin would have viewed with contempt.

It was on religious grounds, even in his earliest years, that Baldwin would begin his turn away from the church. In Part 1, he describes being "bull-whipped" through the Old and New Testaments, all the while taking Job's side and defying God to "talk to *me* from the safety of your whirlwind." Yet something in him, "out of the unbelievable pride and sorrow and beauty of his father's face, caused me to understand ....the fatality and the inexorability of that voice out of the whirlwind, for if one is not able to live with so crushing and continuing a mystery, one is not able to live."[42]

In introducing Baldwin to a religious language, the church ultimately set him free from the church itself, "free ... to live among one's terrors, hour by hour, and day by day, alone, and yet never alone ....To live in connection with a life beyond this life."[43] Under these harrowing spiritual conditions, which account for the sense of urgency in Baldwin's speech and writing, he is able to stay true to the pledge to keep his heart "free of hatred and despair." In a symposium in 1975, he made clear to the audience that he had "kept the faith" that had come to him on the day of his father's funeral. He had ample reason to "hate white people" but due to "mysteries of temperament, luck, and my private history and my sense that hatred is always, in the depths, self-hatred," he did not.[44]

The basis of Baldwin's political radicalism, then, was spiritual and moral. It was because he had to discover for himself the meaning of words like "transgressor" and "evil" that he drew moral conclusions with dangerous political implications.[45] His radicalism also arose from his being an artist, in whom all "action and achievement [rests] on things unseen."[46] It is important to bear in mind that *The Devil Finds Work* is a work of *aesthetic* criticism as much as it is a spiritual and political memoir. Baldwin's interpretation of *The Exorcist*, the most profound section of the book, brilliantly interweaves these strains.

The discussion of *The Exorcist* is preceded by a meditation on Christian "belief," a word that must be placed in quotation marks because it has lost meaning in Western languages, despite the fact that it refers to "a reality." Baldwin is alluding to the survival of a specifically Black Christian faith that originated in the conversion of Africans in the late eighteenth and early nineteenth centuries when Blacks were enslaved:

> The blacks had first been claimed by the Christian church, and then excluded from the company of white Christians—from the fellowship of Christians: which taught us all we needed to know about white Christians. The blacks did not so much use Christian symbols as recognize them for what they were before the Christians came along—and thus reinvested these symbols with their original energy. The proof of this, simply, is the continued existence and authority of the blacks: it is through the creation of the black church that an unwritten, dispersed, and violated inheritance has been handed down.[47]

The Black church is "the custodian" of this inheritance, "which is what blacks have had to be, in Western culture." And to the custodian, "nothing belongs," not even your children; "you must prepare your child to pick up the burden of his life long before the moment when you must lay your burden down."[48]

Over thirty years earlier Baldwin had renounced the belief that the Holy Ghost was speaking through him when he fell on his face before the altar and was prayed over by the "saints" of his church.[49] But he respects the archaic intention of the ritual, which was not to exorcise

Satan, but "to engage Satan in a battle which we knew would never end."[50] This is the crucial difference between the Christian argument of the Black church and that of *The Exorcist*, in which religious dogma is placed in the service of white denial of what evil is. Baldwin emphasizes the film's paranoid focus on domestic invasion and disruption. (There are sounds in the attic and the demon-possessed girl Regan spoils her mother's posh gathering.):

> *The Exorcist* is not in the least concerned with damnation, an abysm far beyond the confines of its imagination, but with property, with safety, tax shelters, stocks and bonds, rising and falling markets, the continued invulnerability of a certain class of people, and the continued sanctification of a certain history. If *The Exorcist* itself believed this history, it could scarcely be reduced to so abject a dependence on special effects.[51]

Baldwin is witty and amusing in describing the special effects of the film, but he is serious about what they imply.

> The mindless and hysterical banality of the evil presented in *The Exorcist* is the most terrifying thing about the film. The American should certainly know more about evil than that; if they pretend otherwise, they are lying, and any black man, and not only blacks—many, many others, including white children, can call them on this lie; he who has been treated *as* the devil recognizes the devil when they meet.

To Baldwin, evil may be found in each of us—and in the mirror. "It is that moment when no other human being is real for you, nor are you real for yourself. This devil has no need of dogma—though he can use them all—nor does he need any historical justification, history being so largely his invention. He does not levitate beds, or fool around with little girls; *we* do."[52] Kafka put this another way: "There can be knowledge of the diabolical, but no belief in it ... "[53]

Nowhere is the "invulnerability of a certain class of people" more clearly implied than at the end of the film, when Regan, who had committed a murder when possessed, departs with her mother, "kisses the Holy Father, and she remembers nothing." *The Devil Finds Work* might have ended here, having illustrated its point so precisely, but in the last paragraph Baldwin takes the discussion to another level by introducing a startling vision:

> The grapes of wrath are stored in the cotton fields and migrant shacks and ghettoes of this nation, and in the schools and prisons, and in the eyes and hearts and perceptions of the wretched everywhere, and in the ruined earth of Vietnam ... these have already kissed the bloody cross and will not bow down before it again: and have forgotten nothing.[54]

Throughout his career Baldwin maintained the principle that the situation of Black people in America cannot be even "discussed coherently" without bearing in mind its history and the mental and moral assumptions upon which all Americans unthinkingly rely.[55] This is why, when questioned during interviews, Baldwin almost always began by addressing the presuppositions behind the question and reminding his listeners of how often he has had to repeat this principle. In a 1968 interview on *The Dick Cavett Show*, Cavett opened by asking Baldwin "Why aren't the Negroes optimistic?" He says that many people believe the situation to be improving considerably, with

Black people now holding positions of influence across society. Cavett asks Baldwin, "Is it at once getting much better and still hopeless?"

In response, Baldwin says, "I don't think there's much hope for it … as long as people are using this peculiar language … It's not a question of what happens to the Negro here, [though] that is a very vivid question for me, but the real question is what's going to happen to this country? I have to repeat that."[56] The story of Blacks in America is the story of America. White Americans pay for what they have permitted by the demoralization of their own lives. No one in America escapes the effects of racism, Baldwin reiterates, and everyone who considers themselves part of the national community "bears some responsibility for it."[57] These words are taken from the opening pages of *Notes of a Native Son*, but their full meaning would not be realized until *The Devil Finds Work*. Baldwin's message "wasn't just hortatory," writes Louis Menand. "He meant it literally ….Anything less than a total social reckoning—a complete psychological makeover of white America—was worthless."[58]

The remarkable thing about Baldwin's life is not only that he kept the pledge he made at nineteen to keep his heart "free of hatred and despair." It's that he did so with little hope for America. This raises the interesting question of whether hope is necessary to living a valid life. Certainly Hollywood would have us believe it is, and offers hope as an opiate. And the Christian church urges its followers to invest hope in an afterlife. But Baldwin says: Beware hope. It can distract us from the truth.

9

Keith Waldrop's *Light While There Is Light*

When Keith Waldrop died in 2023 at the age of ninety, he was known mainly as a prize-winning poet and translator. He had won the National Book Award for Poetry for his 2009 collection *Transcendental Studies: A Trilogy*, and his translations of French poetry and prose were well received. Waldrop also had a growing reputation as a collage artist, having exhibited in solo and group shows in Rhode Island. Yet his one novel, *Light While There Is Light*, garnered little attention when it appeared in 1993. Reissued twenty years later, it was met with a few laudatory reviews but did not gain a wide readership. I should add that the novel has an ambitious subtitle—*An American History*—and that Waldrop considered it his best work.

Waldrop taught at Brown University for four decades and, together with his wife, the poet and translator Rosmarie Waldrop, ran the small non-profit Burning Deck Press from 1961 to 2017. The press gained a reputation as avant-garde, but its list was eclectic. After receiving complaints that the press was not sufficiently programmatic in its taste, the Waldrops wrote:

> Since being eclectic is not always taken for a virtue, we would note that our eclecticism—besides simply reflecting personal ranges of appreciation—is based on an inability to believe that the history of, for instance, poetry can possibly be clear before the poems are written. It is not denying the importance of "movements," to insist that there is another importance in moving beside or apart from them. After all, there are many judgements, none of them the last.[1]

It is worth bearing the above statement in mind when one approaches *Light While There Is Light.* One reason the novel has been neglected is that it is so difficult to categorize. Waldrop seems to take a kind of mischievous pleasure in "moving beside or apart from" the traditions or movements one might be tempted to associate with him. The novel is structured like collage in its use of a dynamic pattern of juxtaposition, but it is also held together by autobiographical narrative. Characters appear and reappear, although we are not always certain that we will meet them again.[2]

There is Waldrop's tormented, evangelical mother, with her delicate hands and mad quest for religious truth; his oddly endearing con artist brothers, who set up a car dealership in Illinois called Used Car Heaven; and minor characters like the college president's little boy Chigger, who murders chicks one by one on the front porch of his house and then howls to be punished. The midwestern and southern towns where the family takes up residence in the mother's search for a religious utopia are so drab that to call them provincial would be to elevate them. At one point, the family lives in Sharon, South Carolina, where Keith attends high school. In 1950, Sharon had a population of 365, but it was near the city of Greenville, where

Bob Jones College, later to become Bob Jones University, was located. From the perspective of Sharon, the family "considered Bob Jones a rather worldly place."[3]

Many years later, Waldrop would become a truly worldly artist whose creations drew on a range of traditions. One senses a multiplicity of literary as well as extra-literary influences beneath the surface of *Light While There Is Light.* According to his students at Brown, Waldrop was a polymath who said that he would rather read than write and who built an extensive library of which literature constituted only a part: "History, archaeology, architecture; epistemology and metaphysics, theology and religion; music; geology, botany, volcanology; psychology, neurophysiology, the study of the brain and the senses" were all represented in Waldrop's library in Providence, according to Jaimy Gordon.[4] Allusions to over half of these subjects find their way seamlessly into *Light While There Is Light.*

On the one hand, Waldrop's novel brings to mind the tradition of American small town life, beginning with Sherwood Anderson's classic group of tales, *Winesburg, Ohio* (1919). In Anderson's portrait of America "society scarcely exists in its legal and affective bonds," John Updike once observed; "dialogue is generally the painful imposition of one monologue upon another."[5] The same might be said of Waldrop's vision of American life. Another reference point is Flannery O'Connor, whose sardonic humor and grotesque characters resonate in Waldrop's evocation of evangelical communities.

On the other hand, there is an undercurrent of nihilism in *Light While There Is Light* that links the novel to European writers like Charles Baudelaire (whom Waldrop translated) and the German writer W.G. Sebald—not a nihilism in which everything is permitted as much as one in which nothing is denied. The novel ends with these words: "As for me, what I would like, I think, is to live a while longer. But not again."[6]

Amusing allusions to American writers appear in the novel. At the Free Methodist church in Emporia, Kansas, which Waldrop attended as a boy, he witnessed the ecstatic demonstrations of two members when they were under the influence of the spirit. They would run up and down the aisles shouting *Amen*, or moan and sink to the floor weeping. "I remember their names as Sister Eliot and Sister Faulkner, though it now sounds unlikely to me," Waldrop drolly interjects. The two sisters are "the natural leaders" of the congregation, just as T.S. Eliot and William Faulkner are perhaps the natural precursors of Waldrop.[7] Eliot was a native of Missouri, although the range of reference in his poetry is vast, and Faulkner, the greatest writer of the American south, portrayed poor, white, agrarian communities that bear a resemblance to some of the communities in Missouri, Kansas, South Carolina, Illinois, and Georgia where Waldrop's family lived. In many ways *Light While There Is Light* is a classic modernist text: it adopts an experimental approach to form and conveys the "shock experience" of contemporary life. There is even a character in the novel called Prophet Shock, perhaps an allusion to Baudelaire.

When we read *Light While There Is Light*, we become conscious of a writer who doesn't claim to understand all he sees. According to Anton Chekhov, this is a virtue in a writer. In the famous letter quoted in Chapter 3, Chekhov wrote:

> It is time for writers ... to admit that you can't figure out anything in this world, as Socrates once admitted and as Voltaire kept

> admitting. The public thinks it knows and understands everything ....However, if an artist whom the public believes decides to state that he understands nothing of what he sees, that in itself is of great significance in the realm of thought and is a great step forward.[8]

The strangely detached tone of Waldrop's novel reflects an underlying acceptance of the incomprehensibility of his subject.

But what is his subject? One can find a buried coming-of-age story in *Light While There Is Light*, but I'm not sure that is its subject. I will begin by describing this story as a way of introducing a few facts about Waldrop's life, which may explain why the word *buried* is appropriate to the way Waldrop's coming of age is represented.

Waldrop's parents, Opal Mohler Waldrop and Arthur Waldrop, came from Missouri and Kansas, part of what is known as the Heartland or Middle America. They were most likely people of German descent, who comprised the largest group of the Midlands since the late 1600s. The Midlands was originally founded by English Quakers, whose belief in the "inner light" and whose sense of sin seem to have acted together with the German Lutheran belief in the Devil to shape Opal's religious opinions. In her religious "pilgrimage" across the Midwest and South, with four children in tow, she became involved in many evangelical groups—local Friends gatherings, the Salvation Army, and the most extreme congregations of the Methodists and Baptists. In Sharon, the congregation the Waldrops joined held street services on a vacant lot where Keith, then a junior high school student, played the violin.

Waldrop describes the pilgrimage as his mother's flight from the unhappiness of her life, explaining that neither "the joys of heaven nor hell's worst prospects provide as forceful a motive as the mere emptiness of the world."[9] Keith's siblings, Charles, Julian, and Elaine, came from the mother's first marriage; the second marriage to Arthur Waldrop, a railroad man twenty years her senior, produced Keith. Both marriages ended in divorce. In the manner of Sebald, Waldrop includes old photographs in the novel. Images of the four siblings and one of Keith together with Charles and his two sons have a way of communicating how close the siblings were, in spite of the immense differences, implied on every page, between Keith and all the others. In the last picture of his mother, her hands cover her face.

A few anecdotes suggest Keith's coming of age as an artist, but only faintly and rather ironically. His father takes him to a mediocre performance of *Hamlet*, which he will never forget. He says that he always intended to write, but never thought of himself as a writer. He takes a graduate course in Henry James and does poorly. Meanwhile, in the manner of Joyce's Stephen Dedalus, he wants to get away from his family. But he doesn't succeed. When he moves to Urbana to begin graduate school, Julian, now being hunted as a deserter from the US Army, and Charles, who has long been out of touch, track him down and move into the dilapidated building he inhabits. They manage to rent part of the first floor where they open Used Car Heaven. (Keith writes the checks for the rent so that Julian cannot be traced, and Charles deals with the state inspector through bribes.) By Keith's second semester, his sister Elaine, her husband Clyde, their infant son, and his mother arrive and move into the second floor. Some of the rooms are separated by curtains and a stove heats the entire building. One wonders what Keith will do in this situation. In a review of the novel, Ben Lerner suggests that we might expect him to at least curse his family, but he seems to accept the situation without a murmur.[10] Lerner quotes this amusing passage:

> One pleasant memory of that stove remains. Julian's blue alley-cat, whom I had named Wozzeck, drank from a bowl behind the stove, and every once in a while practiced what seemed a strange experiment—dipping his paw in the water and then shaking it, so that drops of water, hitting the hot stove, would pop and hiss as they burst into steam. He watched this process with wide green eyes for some time after there was no more reaction, and then, as if in doubt, needing further proof, would try it again. Sometimes this went on for half an hour. I could see it from my bed, where he slept also.[11]

Like many a fairytale hero who in his youth sleeps by the stove, has communion with animals, and appears lazy and idle while his unscrupulous brothers make their way through trickery, Keith will, after many trials, achieve success.

Eventually Julian is arrested and imprisoned and Charles marries a prostitute named Seely, who later succumbs to madness. Over the years, all members of the family except Keith become increasingly paranoid and susceptible to charlatans. Julian marries a woman known as the "Prophetess" who possibly brings about his death. In her final years Keith's mother refuses to live with anyone and rents a one-car garage with a toilet and sink installed in a corner. She lives on "fishwiches" from the fast-food drive-in next door, whipping cream, and grapefruit. When she is dying, one of the five patients who share the hospital room with her shouts, "Jesus! … Jesus you bastard!—why won't you let me die?"[12]

For Waldrop, existence cannot be either rationalized or justified, hence the collage structure that colorfully and dramatically destabilizes the autobiographical narrative. This narrative is not always chronological, and pieces of it are juxtaposed with philosophical speculations that invite us to see Waldrop's life in a constantly shifting pattern of departure and return, both mental and physical. Reason has a place in the narrative because, to Waldrop's chagrin, the people closest to him have abandoned it. The harrowing trajectories of the lives of his mother and brothers show us very clearly what happens when people have nothing to measure their experience but the intensity of their inner lives. Keith's mother decides to move the children to Sharon after she intuits that a suitor of Elaine's is possessed. "This was the sign that pointed us to Sharon."[13]

A break in the narrative follows immediately upon this revelation, creating the sort of suggestive juxtaposition characteristic of collage. Waldrop reminisces about a dinner party that presumably took place years later when he was teaching at Brown. For the entire evening, Keith and Rosmarie listen politely to a philosopher pontificating on the notion of divine omnipotence. The miracles of the Bible, the philosopher claims, violate the laws of nature, "but these laws are based on observation, and merely empirical, and deity is above them." Human beings cannot perform miracles, but God can. He is omnipotent and can do anything—except violate the laws of logic:

> Even God cannot annul the law of identity, which says that whatever is, is. He can, of course, destroy what is, but cannot make it at the same time be and not be. He can create seven times seventy

> worlds, but cannot keep seven from being a prime number. Two plus two equals four in all possible worlds, created or uncreated.

Waldrop muses:

> Well, I had heard all this before, and while he was talking, and on the way home, I was faintly amused by anyone taking such things seriously. But later that night I was unreasonably angry, to think that people professing belief in God should turn and subject Him to Copi or Quine. If I were to invent a god, I would make sure he didn't get stuck with the primeness of seven or have reason to feel threatened by Gödel's proof. He might produce a square circle, if he felt so inclined. And, yes, he could, at one and the same moment, exist and not exist.[14]

However strange Waldrop's mother's behavior may seem, the professor's complacency is stranger still. Waldrop's conclusion that God could, "at one and the same moment, exist and not exist" places him closer to his mother's superstition than to the professor's foolish rationalism.

"All my family … have a streak of the unworldly. For us, God's sphere of action and the local scene rarely make contact ….Once in a while, however, a spark manages to pass from one sphere to the other."[15] The near-absolute separation of the human from the divine is perhaps the most compelling philosophical and moral theme in *Light While There Is Light*. It accounts for the suffering of innocent characters, including two deaths that border on negligent homicide. The death of a girl named Evangeline is brought about through her "condemnation" in the Sharon congregation. In having been born before her mother converted to Christianity, she is placed forever outside God's mercy. Waldrop does not need to know the specific cause of her death, which remains unclear, in order to contemplate her persecution:

> When I try to think of her dying … I find myself somehow with an image of the Piazza San Marco. Saint Mark's lion flaps in the wind. Pigeons resting on the frieze of Napoleon's Wing appear as irregular dots on bright filigree. God in shards, shining with gold leaf, receives with absolutely no expression the news of Abel's murder.[16]

Elsewhere in the novel, Waldrop writes that he is an "unbeliever."[17] One thinks here of Simone Weil's characterization of the atheist as someone who is angry at God.

The second death, that of Julian, seems to have been brought about by his wife Kate, the Prophetess. In his final years Julian is in poor health and on insulin for diabetes, but since Kate got him to believe that true Christians need not suffer death, he stops taking care of himself and even goes off insulin for periods. There is a suggestion that Kate profits financially from his death. Two months after the funeral, she remarries.

Waldrop's religio-philosophical interjections seem randomly placed, but they undergird a devastating reality: that terrible consequences can result when people decide they have personal access to divine knowledge and are called upon to regulate the souls around them. If anything distinguishes Waldrop's family from the evangelicals who exploit them, it's their curiosity, a trait Waldrop shares.

The darkness of the stories involving Evangeline, Julian, and others does not overwhelm the reader because sparks of Waldrop's humor light up enough sentences and scenes to distract us from what is taking place. When Julian gets out of prison for desertion, he tells Keith "he felt he had gotten a bargain—he would have had another year and a half in the air force. The hardest moment to get through, he said, was at the end when, being told solemnly that he would never again be allowed to serve in the armed forces of the United States, he knew he absolutely must not laugh."[18]

And there is the family's effort to connect with the spirit realm through the Ouiji board when they gather as adults over holidays: "It got so every night the board was talking to them. While the Christmas tree turned into a pile of needles, they tested their discovery . . . . 'Where are my pliers?' Clyde asked, and the answer spelled itself out: 'B-E-H-I-N-D-T-V,' which is where they were. It never seemed to miss on little things like that." More serious questions about family history lead to the intimation that one branch of the family ended with Mad King Ludwig of Bavaria.

At one point Julian asks the genie about Keith's wife: "What about Rosmarie?" Waldrop writes: "And this should be noted: the Genie of Old never answered any questions about Rosmarie. She was, as it were, outside his jurisdiction."[19] This is evidently a Waldrop family genie, or at least one that knows its audience.

Light While There Is Light is informed by a modesty that runs as deep as its philosophical curiosity. Perhaps this is another reason, in addition to the novel's uncategorizable status, that it has received little attention. The reading public is not inclined to celebrate modest works of genius that teeter on their own philosophical uncertainty. It prefers bombastic creations like Barbara Kingsolver's extravagantly promoted *Demon Copperhead*, a novel that exemplifies the sort of know-it-all style Chekhov disliked. Set in Appalachia among poor families and desperate circumstances, Kingsolver's novel announces on every page the author's overweening confidence that she has the world figured out.

In contrast, Waldrop's style is restrained by his own cat-like curiosity. In his portrait of the repeated relocations and social isolation of his youth, conditions that many Americans experience, he does not deny the horror and humor of what he sees, but he never strives for these effects. In his signature detachment, every sentence becomes a palimpsest of emotions, a moment both felt and observed. And each of these moments figures in a collage of incidents and speculations that are as vivid and precise as the lines in a poem. One may wonder how such an idiosyncratic sensibility—impassioned, superstitious, whimsical—came into being. As Wilde said, we have ancestors in literature as in life, and Waldrop's literary forebears are an unlikely bunch: Baudelaire, Faulkner, O'Connor, Sebald. Moreover, Waldrop said that in his early years he read only the Bible and comic books. It is no wonder, then, that he was "capable of being in uncertainties, mysteries, doubts."[20] This is where the artist naturally dwells, according to Keats's famous description, but few artists have been more at ease there than Keith Waldrop.

NOTES

Introduction

1 Michel Houllebecq, *Whatever*, trans. Paul Hammond (London: Serpent's Tail, 1998), 40. First published in French as *Extension du domaine de la lutte* in 1994.

2 Charles Dickens, *Our Mutual Friend* (New York: New American Library, [1864–5] 1964), 20–1.

3 Aristotle, *Aristotle's Poetics* (New York: Hill and Wang, 1961), 65. Translation modified.

4 I echo here a well-known statement by Henry James: "What is character but the determination of incident? What is incident but the illustration of character?" See James, "The Art of Fiction [1884]," *The Portable Henry James*, ed. Morton Zabel (New York: Viking, 1956), 401.

5 Michel Houellebecq, *The Elementary Particles*, trans. Frank Wynne (New York: Vintage, 2001). First published in French as *Les Particules élémentaires* in 1998.

6 In "The Moral Scope of the English *Bildungsroman*" I elaborate on the ethical continuity of the English novel tradition. See Brown, "The Moral Scope of the English *Bildungsroman*," *The Oxford Handbook of the Victorian Novel*, ed. Lisa Rodensky (Oxford: Oxford University Press, 2013), 663–78.

7 Milan Kundera, *The Art of the Novel*, trans. Linda Asher (New York: Harper & Row, 1986), 5–6.

8 Kevin Lozano, "How Has Big Publishing Changed American Fiction?" *The New Yorker* (November 1, 2023). https://www.newyorker.com/books/under-review/how-has-big-publishing-changed-american-fiction. The essay is a review of Dan Sinykin's *Big Fiction: How Conglomeration Changed the Publishing Industry and American Literature* (New York: Columbia University Press, 2023).

9 Lozano online.

10 As Zadie Smith points out in her influential review-essay, "Two Paths for the Novel," literary Realism is still the dominant mode in fiction today. Contemporary publishing houses tend to be "less aware (or less interested) in seeing what's new" in avant-garde writing. See "Two Paths for the Novel," *NYRB* 55, no. 18 (November 20, 2008): 94.

11 In *Immediacy or, The Style of Too Late Capitalism* (London: Verso, 2024) Anna Kornbluh mentions many autofiction writers, including Karl Ove Knausgaard and Rachel Cusk, whose writing constitutes a "revolt against character, form, and fictionality itself" (71). To Kornbluh, this transformation in the history of the novel during the twenty-first century is a reflection of "economic restructuring in the anglophone world….Economic premiums on speed, flow, and auto-actualization inscribe themselves into literary style; immediacy writing's anti-representational, anti-fictional centrifugality of charisma aestheticizes this capitalist base" (81–2). See also Sinykin's description of the way today's autofiction differs from earlier literature that uses the author's self in a work of fiction: "Just because autofiction is old…does not mean its mode of deployment is unchanged. That it has a new name ought to tip us off. It, for one, is another kind of genre play that makes a bid for a large readership under the current market dispensation" (Sinykin, *Big Fiction*, 18).

12 Patricia Lockwood, *No One Is Talking about This* (New York: Riverhead Books, 2021), 98.

13 Stylistic studies, after long neglect, appears to be having a resurgence. See the work of Garrett Stewart, especially *Style in Fiction* (Cambridge: Cambridge University Press, 2018) and *The Ways of the Word: Episodes in Verbal Attention* (Ithaca: Cornell University Press, 2022). A renewed appreciation of the importance of character has also been growing in literary studies. See the Introduction of *Character: Three Inquiries of Literary Studies* by Amanda Anderson, Rita Felski, and Toril Moi (Chicago and London: University of Chicago Press, 2019), 1–25.

14 See Rita Felski's *The Limits of Critique* (Chicago: University of Chicago Press, 2016) and "Introduction," *Critique and Postcritique*, ed. Elizabeth S. Anker and Rita Felski (Durham and London: Duke University Pres, 2017), 1–28.

Chapter 1

1 Michel Houellebecq, *Whatever*, trans. Paul Hammond (London: Serpent's Tail, 1998), 40. First published in French as *Extension du domaine de la lutte* in 1994.

2 In 2005 a new anthology of modernism edited by Lawrence Rainey appeared, hailed on the book jacket as "the most comprehensive of Anglo-American modernism ever to be published." The anthology comes to 1,216 pages and includes selections from scores of modernists, including a great many lesser-known writers like Wyndham Lewis and Mina Loy. There are no selections from D.H. Lawrence. See Rainey, ed., *Modernism: An Anthology* (New Jersey: Wiley-Blackwell, 2005).

3 "Burbank," "Gerontion," "Sweeney among the Nightingales," "A Cooking Egg," and the posthumously published "Dirge" are among the poems by T.S. Eliot most often cited for their anti-semitic content. In "Gerontion" Eliot writes: "My house is a decayed house, / And the jew squats on the window sill, the owner, / Spawned in some estaminet of Antwerp, /Blistered in Brussels, patched and peeled in London" (*The Wasteland and Other Poems* [New York: Harcourt, Brace & World, 1962], 19). See Christopher Ricks' *T.S. Eliot and Prejudice* for an insightful analysis of the question of Eliot's prejudice (Berkeley: University of California Press, 1989). Pound's sympathy with fascism is well known. As a collaborator in Fascist Italy during the Second World War, he delivered viciously anti-semitic radio broadcasts between 1939 and 1945.

4 Gary Adelman, *Reclaiming D.H.Lawrence: Contemporary Writers Speak Out* (London: Associated University Presses, 2002). I am indebted to Adelman's book for its extensive review of the thoughts of twentieth-century writers on Lawrence. My discussion of students' responses to Lawrence differs from that of Adelman in being focused less on their ideological objections than their antipathy to Lawrence's characters and worldview, both of which are colored by his singular religiosity.

5 Ibid., 31–2.

6 D.H. Lawrence, "The Horse-Dealer's Daughter," *The Complete Short Stories*, vol. 2 (New York: Viking, 1961), 448.

7 Ibid., 449.

8 Ibid., 452.

9 Ibid., 454.

10 Ibid., 455.

11 Ibid., 456–7.

12 John Tytell, "D.H. Lawrence and Frieda," *Passionate Lives* (New York: Carol Publishing Group, 1991), 64.

13 D.H. Lawrence, *Women in Love* (New York: Viking Press, 1960), 99–100. Given scenes like this one, it comes as no surprise that Lawrence's novels figure in works of ecocriticism. In *A Century of Early Ecocriticism,* David Mazel claims Lawrence as an early ecocritic. (See Mazel, *A Century of Early Ecocriticism* [Athens: University of Georgia Press, 2001], 11.) See also Rachel Murray's *Modernist Exoskeleton: Insects, War, Literary Form* (Edinburgh: Edinburgh University Press, 2020), which includes *Lady Chatterley's Lover* in its exploration of modernist writers' attention to nonhuman life. Many of the writers quoted in Adelman praise Lawrence for his natural description.

14 Benjamin Kunkel, "The Deep End," *The New Yorker* (December 11, 2005). https://www.newyorker.com/magazine/2005/12/19/the-deep-end

15 D.H. Lawrence, "A Propos of Lady Chatterley's Lover," *Sex, Literature, and Censorship* (New York: Viking Press, 1959), 109.

16 Lawrence, *Women in Love,* 347–8.

17 William Wordsworth, "The World Is too Much with Us," *The Norton Anthology of English Literature,* 8th edition, vol. D, ed. Stephen Greenblatt and M.H. Abrams (New York: W.W. Norton, 2006), 319.

18 In my discussion of Lawrence's style here, I draw attention to some of the excesses in the prose of his essays; examples of excess may be found in the novels as well. But for a dazzling appreciation of Lawrence's style, see Garrett Stewart's analysis of the erotic prose of *Women in Love* in *Style in Fiction* (Cambridge: Cambridge University Press, 2018) which tracks the "rhapsodic deconstruction" of being that takes place linguistically, as the grammar of Lawrence's sentences disintegrates (94). See also Stewart's analysis of the conclusion of *The Rainbow* in *The Ways of the Word: Episodes in Verbal Attention* (Ithaca: Cornell University Press, 2022) in which "wonder is maintained at the level of style's own layering, shades of purple prose included" (159).

19 D.H. Lawrence, "Cocksure Men and Hensure Women," *Sex, Literature, and Censorship* (New York: Viking Press, 1959), 47.

20 D.H. Lawrence, *Lady Chatterley's Lover* (New York: New American Library, 1959), 42–3.

21 Ibid., 65.

22 Kate Millett, *Sexual Politics* (New York: Doubleday, 1970), 238. Lawrence discusses "phallic marriage" in "A Propos of *Lady Chatterley's Lover*," 102.

23 Lawrence, *Lady Chatterley's Lover*, 237.

24 Millett, *Sexual Politics*, 238. Regarding Millett, who was my teacher in college, I should add that one of her strengths as a critic was a sense of humor, a quality that critics of her work generally ignored.

25 Lawrence, "A Propos of *Lady Chatterley's Lover*," 106–7.

26 Ibid., 100.

27 Ibid., 102.

28 Ibid., 103.

29 Lawrence, "The Horse-Dealer's Daughter," 447.

30 D.H. Lawrence, "The Odour of Chrysanthemums," *The Complete Short Stories*, vol. 2 (New York: Viking, 1961), 300–1.

31 Lawrence, "A Propos of *Lady Chatterley's Lover*," 87.

Chapter 2

1 See James Wolcott's "Sisyphus at the Selectric," *London Review of Books* 43, no. 10 (2021): 3–10. In a letter to the editor in response to its misrepresentation, I wrote the following: "In speculations about a possible 'affinity' between Philip Roth and his biographer Blake Bailey, James Wolcott cites Roth's foreword to Frederica Wagman's *Playing House* (1973), a novel about sibling incest. In a footnote Wolcott showcases a quotation which, taken out of context and accompanied by Wolcott's response ('In the immortal words of Ethel Merman, "Jesus Christ"'), implies that Roth endorses the horrific sexual acts depicted in Wagman's work. I urge readers to consult Roth's foreword, which is included in his collection of essays and reviews *Reading Myself and Others* (1975). The quotation Wolcott cites merely summarizes the perspective of Wagman's narrator. Roth then goes on to suggest that what is so extraordinary about the novel is that the point of view 'is not Humbert Humbert's but Lolita's—only a Lolita with heart and nerves exposed, a little girl at once more ordinary and more loving, and, for that reason, more profoundly destroyed.' Roth ends the review with the statement: 'The only irony Frederica Wagman's heroine is able to know is the irony of her enslavement; she is beyond everyone's reach, poor woman, except the one who touched her first.'" (Brown, "Letters," *LRB* 43, no. 12 [2021]: 4.)

2 Two popular contemporary novels discussed in Ch. 3—Celeste Ng's *Our Missing Hearts* (New York: Penguin, 2022) and Kamala Shamsie's *Home Fire* (New York: Riverhead, 2017)—contain highly idealized heroines, but the characters do not resonate with the history of fiction in the way the heroine of *When She Was Good* resonates.

3 Philip Roth, *When She Was Good* (New York: Random House, 1967), 82.

4 Ibid., 277.

5 Qtd. in Blake Bailey, *Philip Roth: The Biography* (New York: W.W. Norton, 2021), 281.

6 An important exception was Raymond Rosenthal's review in *The New Leader*, which characterized Roth as a modernist influenced by Flaubert: "Roth has written the most violently satiric book about American life since [...] Evelyn Waugh's *The Loved One*" (qtd. in Bailey, *Philip Roth*, 282).

7 Qtd. in Bailey, *Philip Roth*, 656.

8 Roth, *When She Was Good*, 3.

9 Ibid., 83.

10 Roth's title is taken from Longfellow's nursery rhyme, "There Was a Little Girl." The first stanza reads: "There was a little girl, / Who had a little curl, / Right in the middle of her forehead. / When she was good, / She was very good indeed, / But when she was bad she was horrid."

11 Harold Bloom, *Jane Austen* (New York: Chelsea House, 1986), 11–12.

12 Ibid., 10.

13 Qtd. in Bailey, *Philip Roth*, 448.

14 Oscar Wilde, "Preface to *The Picture of Dorian Gray*," *The Artist as Critic: Critical Writings of Oscar Wilde*, ed. Richard Ellmann (Chicago: University of Chicago Press, 1968), 235.

Chapter 3

1 The style of popular fiction I am describing derives in part from the dominant style of contemporary culture—that of "immediacy," according to Anna Kornbluh. Kornbluh writes: "The paradox of immediacy is a cultural style that imagines itself unstyled" (Anna Kornbluh, *Immediacy: Or, The Style of Too Late Capitalism* [London: Verso, 2024], 11).

2 Celeste Ng, *Our Missing Hearts* (New York: Penguin, 2022).

3 Kamila Shamsie, *Home Fire* (New York: Riverhead, 2017).

4 Henry James, "The Art of Fiction [1884]," *The Portable Henry James*, ed. Morton Zabel (New York: Viking, 1956), 401. See also Aristotle, *Aristotle's Poetics*, trans. S.H. Butcher (New York: Hill and Wang, 1961), 22; 62–3; 65.

5 Milan Kundera, *The Art of the Novel*, trans. Linda Asher (New York: Harper & Row, 1986).

6 A well-known example from the record we have of Austen's manner of conceiving character relates to *Emma*. "I am going to take a heroine whom no one but myself will much like," she confided when she began the novel (Jane Austen, *Emma* [New York: W.W. Norton, (1815) 1993], x). Becky Sharp, the heroine of Thackeray's *Vanity Fair*, is based on a composite of women Thackeray knew or had heard about.

7 The study of character appears to be enjoying a resurgence in literary studies. See *Character: Three Inquiries in Literary Study* (Chicago and London: University of Chicago Press, 2019) by Amanda Anderson, Rita Felski, and Toril Moi for arguments against the view that attention to character merely embraces outmoded theories of the subject. In their explorations of what character criticism can illuminate, the authors call into question some of the assumptions that have dominated literary studies in recent decades.

8 Devina Heriyanto, "Interview: Kamila Shamsie Talks about 'Home Fire,' Minorities and Terrorism," *The Jakarta Post* (April 4, 2018). https://www.thejakartapost.com/life/2018/04/04/interview-kamila-shamsie-talks-about-home-fire-minorities-and-terrorism.html

9 In this chapter I do not extend my introductory discussion of the impact that the conglomeration of the publishing industry has had on contemporary popular fiction because I want to retain a focus on the novels themselves. I wish only to point out here that it is difficult not to conclude that the pressures of mass marketing played a role in shaping Ng's and Shamsie's

fiction. See Sinykin's *Big Fiction: How Conglomeration Changed the Publishing Industry and American Literature,* especially Chapter 1: Mass Market (I): How Mass-Market Books Changed Publishing (23-46) and Chapter 4: Trade (II): How Literary Writers Embraced Genre (100-25).

10 See the discussion of the idea of agency as a philosophical and political concept in James Griffin, *On Human Rights* (Oxford: Oxford University Press, 2008), 44–5, 67–8.

11 "Agency," Gender Equity Toolbox. Bill and Melinda Gates Foundation. https://www.gatesgenderequalitytoolbox.org/measuring-empowerment/agency/

12 See Aristotle, *Aristotle's Poetics*, 61–6.

13 Ng, *Our Missing Hearts*, 327.

14 Milan Kundera, *The Unbearable Lightness of Being*, trans. Michael Henry Heim (New York: Harper & Row, 1984), 75.

15 Ibid., 184.

16 Morgan Talty, *The Night of the Living Rez* (Portland: Tin House, 2022), 35.

17 Ibid., 52.

18 Ibid., 45.

19 Ibid., 50.

20 Amil Niazi, "Beer Runs, Porcupine Hunts, Jars of Teeth and Much More," *New York Times* (July 1, 2022). https://www.nytimes.com/2022/07/01/books/review/night-of-the-living-rez-morgan-talty.html. According to a recent report from Harvard University, Penobscots and other tribes in Maine are even more disadvantaged than most other Native communities in the United States.

21 Niazi online.

22 See Sinykin for a discussion of the role played by the publishing industry in the awarding of prizes (44-5).

23 Colm Tóibín, *The Magician* (New York: Scribner, 2021).

24 An example of how the questionable portrait of Mann impacts the plot of *The Magician* may be seen in the chapters when Mann escapes to Switzerland with his family in 1933. Tóibín suggests that Mann was overwhelmed with anxiety over the possible discovery of diaries left behind in Munich containing homosexual fantasies, even though Mann had openly explored such fantasies in *Death in Venice,* published in 1912. It seems more likely that Mann would have been most preoccupied during these weeks with his own safety and that of his children, in-laws, and friends, some of whom had remained in Germany. The chapters involving this period in *The Magician* are taken up with Mann's fearful erotic recollections of a young man he had met named Klaus Heuser, whom he described in the diaries. The lengthy episode about Heuser interrupts the suspense of Mann's escape from Germany with an inward-turning digression and invites the reader to accept a somewhat unconvincing portrait of a man in such circumstances.

25 Anton Chekhov, "Selections from Chekhov's Letters," *Anton Chekhov's Short Stories*, ed. and trans. Ralph Matlaw (New York: Norton, 1979), 270.

26 Colm Tóibín, Interview, "A Ghost in His Own Life: Colm Tóibín on the Great Thomas Mann," *Radio Open Source* (October 1, 2021). https://lithub.com/a-ghost-in-his-own-life-colm-toibin-on-the-great-thomas-mann/

27 The differences between realistic and experimental fiction are at issue in this chapter only insofar as they further illustrate Kundera's point that character is the enduring basis of the novel form. The novelist who experiments with character experiments with form; Lockwood is an excellent example of this because her experiments with the narrator of *No One Is Talking about This* determine the avant-garde structure of the novel. In "Two Paths for the Novel," Smith discusses the two great traditions—literary realism and avant-garde fiction—and ends the essay by drawing attention to the "revealing points of connection" between them: "At their crossroads we find extraordinary writers claimed by both sides: Melville, Conrad, Kafka, Becket, Joyce, Nabokov" (Smith, "Two Paths for the Novel," *NYRB* 55, no. 18 [November 20, 2008]: 94). Recalling the structure of the foundational European novel, Cervantes' *Don Quixote* (1605, 1615), one could argue that the novel genre itself is rooted in a kind of double vision, a sustained attention to what is both realistically probable and utterly fantastical and dreamlike. In "The Depreciated Legacy of Cervantes," Kundera lays claim to this inheritance and places Cervantes at the center of the European tradition (*The Art of the Novel*, 3–20). In "Two Paths for the Novel," Smith focuses on the Anglo-American tradition in which realist fiction is dominant, but a large part of the review-essay is given over to highlighting a recent work of avant-garde fiction, Tom McCarthy's *Remainder*. Smith's evaluation of the realist novel under review (Joseph O'Neill's *Netherland*) is less positive. She suggests that the type of lyrical realism it represents is so perfectly executed that it amounts to an assault on the tradition, in the way that photography brought about a crisis in painted portraiture. Smith finds in the experiments of *Remainder* more hope for the future of the novel: "It clears away a little of the dead wood, offering a glimpse of an alternate road down which the novel might, with difficulty, travel forward. We could call this constructive deconstruction, a quality that, for me, marks *Remainder* as one of the great English novels of the past ten years" (Smith, "Two Paths for the Novel," 94). While the avant-garde fiction appearing today speaks well for the future of the novel, I believe both traditions are producing powerful and innovative work, as my admiration for both Talty and Lockwood suggests.

28 Patricia Lockwood, *No One Is Talking about This* (New York: Riverhead Books, 2021), 198.

29 Ibid., 119.

30 Ibid., 94.

31 Ibid., 98.

Chapter 4

1 Aristotle, "Politics," *The Basic Works of Aristotle*, ed. Richard McKeon (New York: Random House, 1966), 1257b. I am following the standard citation practice for Aristotle and employing Bekker numbers to indicate the location of specific quotations.

2 Max Weber, *The Protestant Ethic and the Spirit of Capitalism*, ed. Richard Swedberg (New York and London: W.W. Norton, 2009), 28.

3 For a more detailed analysis of the contradictions in Defoe's narrative, see Brown, "Robinson Crusoe's 'Tent Upon the Earth,'" *Journal of Architecture* 43, no. 4 (2008): 365–78.

4 The economic concerns of the English novel have been treated extensively in literary criticism for decades. This is true of all the major novels discussed in this chapter. To give one example: a critical tradition that focuses on economics in Austen's novels may be traced from Mark Shorer's ground-breaking essay of 1948 on Austen's pervasive use of mercantile language ("Technique as Discovery," *Hudson Review* Vol. 1, 1) on up to Ruth Perry's influential 2004 analysis of Austen in *Novel Relations: The Transformation of Kinship in English Literature and Culture (1748–1818)* and beyond. (Perry examines the impact of the development of a market economy on Austen's conception of marriage). There are also extensive bibliographies on these novelists outside England and America, such as the Marxist tradition of

Dickens criticism in Russia. The aim of this essay is not to advance research on any one novel but to examine the experience of monetary wealth in a range of English novels.

5 In an earlier essay I discuss the continuity of the English novel tradition and how questions of class and money often figure in novels that focus on the theme of accountability. See Brown, "The Moral Scope of the English *Bildungsroman*," *The Oxford Handbook of the Victorian Novel*, ed. Lisa Rodensky (Oxford: Oxford University Press, 2013), 663–78.

6 A.H. Clough, "As I Sat at the Cafe, I Said to Myself," *Victorian Poetry and Poetics*, ed. G. Walter Houghton and Robert E. Stange (Boston: Houghton Mifflin, 1959), 348.

7 Aristotle, "Nicomachean Ethics," *The Basic Works of Aristotle*, ed. Richard McKeon (New York: Random House, 1966), 1122b7.

8 Jane Austen, *Emma* (New York and London: W.W. Norton, 2012), 5.

9 Charles Dickens, *Great Expectations* (New York and London: W.W. Norton, 1999), 115.

10 Ibid., 346.

11 Ibid., 87.

12 Clough, "As I Sat at the Cafe, I Said to Myself," 348.

13 Anthony Trollope, *Barchester Towers* (Leicester: Isis Clear Type Classics, 1990), 181.

Chapter 5

1 See Richard Ellmann, "A Late Victorian Love Affair," *Oscar Wilde* (New York: Alfred A. Knopf, 1988), 384–407.

2 For my discussion of Wilde's life and of his attitude toward his sexuality as it relates to his aesthetics, see Brown, *Cosmopolitan Criticism: Oscar Wilde's Philosophy of Art* (Charlottesville and London: University Press of Virginia, 1997), 1–23.

3 Oscar Wilde, *Selected Letters of Oscar Wilde*, ed. Rupert Hart-David (Oxford: Oxford University Press, 1979), 348.

4 Helen Vendler, *The Music of What Happens* (Cambridge: Harvard University Press, 1988), 286.

5 William Butler Yeats, *The Autobiography of William Butler Yeats* (New York: Macmillan, 1965), 189.

6 H. Montgomery Hyde and Oscar Wilde, *A Biography* (New York: Farrar, Strauss and Giroux, 1975), 204.

7 Ellmann, "A Late Victorian Love Affair," 523.

8 Brown, *Cosmopolitan Criticism*, 22.

9 Ellmann, "A Late Victorian Love Affair," 578.

10 Diane Johnson, *The True History of the First Mrs. Meredith and Other Lesser Lives* (New York: New York Review Books, 1972), 216.

11 Ibid., 138.

12 Oscar Wilde, *The Artist as Critic: Critical Writings of Oscar Wilde*, ed. Richard Ellmann (Chicago: University of Chicago Press, 1968), 305.

13 Ellmann, "A Late Victorian Love Affair," 429.

14 See Joan Acocella, "A Hard Case," *Twenty-Eight Artists and Two Saints* (New York: Pantheon, 2007), 99; 108. I draw on Acocella's essay in my comments here. The essay is a review of Carole Angier's 2002 biography of Levi, *The Double Bond: Primo Levi, a Biography.* (New York: Farrar, Straus and Giroux, 2002).

15 See Acocella, "A Hard Case," 108–10.

16 John Updike, "Reflections: Kafka's Short Stories," *The New Yorker* (May 9, 1983), 121.

17 Franz Kafka, *The Metamorphosis*, trans. Stanley Corngold (New York and London: W.W. Norton, 1996), 3.

18 Ibid., 4.

19 Ibid., 11.

20 Ibid., 15.

21 Jean Collignon, "Kafka's Humor," *Foray through Existentialism, Yale French Studies* 16 (1955): 54. See also pp. 53–4 for a discussion of the nature of Kafka's humor, and how it does not correspond to others kinds of humor, such as that found in Rabelais or Fielding.

22 Walter Benjamin, Letter to Gershom Scholem, June 12, 1938, *The Correspondence of Walter Benjamin and Gershom Scholem*, ed. Gershom Scholem (New York: Schocken Books, 1989), 225.

23 Thomas Mann, "Homage," *The Castle* (New York: Alfred A. Knopf, 1968), x; xvi.

24 Collignon, "Kafka's Humor," 60.

25 Mann, "Homage," x.

Chapter 6

1 Victoria Glendinning, *Anthony Trollope* (New York: Alfred A. Knopf, 1993), 469.

2 Ibid., 381.

3 Jake Bittle, "Stuck in the Middle: The Quiet Radicalism of Anthony Trollope's Palliser Novels," *The Nation* (February 20, 2020). https://www.thenation.com/article/culture/trollope-palliser-novels-centrism-essay/

4 Anthony Trollope, *The Eustace Diamonds* (Oxford and New York: Oxford University Press, 1983), 125.

5 Adam Gopnick, "Trollope Trending," *The New Yorker* (April 27, 2015). https://www.newyorker.com/magazine/2015/05/04/trollope-trending

6 Anthony Trollope, *The Warden* (Surrey: Alma Classics, 2020), 25.

7 See, for example, the opening chapters of Dickens' *Oliver Twist* for repeated use of the words "system" and "systematic" in reference to the administrative structures of the New Poor Law.

8 Anthony Trollope, *The Small House at Allington* (London and New York: Everyman's Library, 1965), 548.

9 Ibid., 554.

10 W.H. Auden, "A Poet of the Actual," *Forewords and Afterwords* (New York: Vintage Books, 1990), 265.

11 In this respect, Trollope's novels may be said to illustrate very well what French sociologist Pierre Bourdieu, drawing on Marx, called "social reproduction" or the process by which society reproduces the same social

structures and systems from generation to generation. See Bourdieu, *Distinction: A Social Critique of the Judgement of Taste* (Cambridge: Harvard University Press, 1984).

12 Trollope, *The Warden*, 161.

Chapter 7

1 See Vicki Kunkel's *Instant Appeal* (New York: Amacom Books, 2008) and Steve Salerno's *SHAM: How the Self-Help Movement Made America Helpless* (New York: Crown Publishing Group, 2005), both of which question the efficacy of self-help and motivational literature.

2 Beth Blum's *The Self-Help Compulsion: Searching for Advice in Modern Literature* (New York: Columbia University Press, 2020) offers historical perspective on self-help literature from the nineteenth century to the present. In a discussion of the Victorian period, for example, Blum points to the politically radical roots of the self-help genre and shows how it was transformed by the values of laissez-faire capitalism, particularly in Smiles's *Self-Help*. Blum also analyzes the complex relations between self-help literature and literary fiction, showing how both can spring from similar efforts to deal with the pressures of experience at a given moment in history. Overall, her book examines self-help as a mode of writing and also as a mode of reading: the desire to find in literature pointers on how to live is ancient.

3 Thomas Carlyle, *Sartor Resartus* (Oxford and New York: Oxford University Press, [1833–34] 1987), 124.

4 Ibid., 127.

5 *Sartor Resartus* was first published in 1833–4. The title literally means "The Tailor Re-Patched." Stefan Collini's 2023 essay on Carlyle in the *London Review of Books* discusses the decline of Carlyle's influence. See Collini, "Mainly Puddling," *London Review of Books* 45, no. 24 (2023): 43–4.

6 Carlyle, *Sartor Resartus,* 88.

7 Ibid., 128.

8 Ibid., 128–9.

9 Ibid., 129.

10 *The Wizard of Oz*. Dir. Victor Fleming. MGM, 1939. DVD. Criterion Collection.

11 Joseph Conrad, *Lord Jim* (Toronto: Broadview Literary Texts, 2001), 180.

12 Carlyle, *Sartor Resartus*, 126.

13 Arthur C. Brooks and Oprah Winfrey, *Build the Life You Want: The Art and Science of Getting Happier* (New York: Portfolio/Penguin, 2023), 116–17.

14 John Stuart Mill, *Autobiography* (Boston: Houghton Mifflin, 1969), 85.

15 The ubiquitous goal of happiness is immediately evident in the subtitles of many self-help books. Two examples may be seen in books I refer to in this essay: *From Strength to Strength: Finding Success, Happiness, and Deep Purpose in the Second Half of Life* by Arthur C. Brooks (New York: Portfolio/Penguin, 2022), and *Love Your Enemies: How to Break the Anger Habit & Be a Whole Lot Happier* by Sharon Salzberg and Robert Thurman (California: Hay House, Inc., 2013). The authors of these works do not deny the problems traditionally associated with seeking happiness directly. Both books have wisdom to offer, but they are typical of self-help literature in dangling the possibility of unalloyed happiness as an incentive both to buy the book and read it to the end so as to know all its secrets. Brooks published another self-help book, cited above, which he wrote with Oprah Winfrey, one year after *From Strength to Strength*. In the second book he makes a reasoned case for not making happiness the goal of life, but not before he describes an ecstatically happy man. The man is a professor giving a lecture who is so full of joy that he grins "from ear to ear" and does push-ups on the stage despite the fact he is dying of pancreatic cancer (Brooks and Winfrey, *Build the Life You Want*, 1).

16 A conservative strain in contemporary self-help literature, in which more direct confrontations with oneself are urged upon the reader, is exemplified in Jordan Peterson's popular *12 Rules for Life: An Antidote to Chaos* (Toronto: Penguin Random House Canada, 2018).

17 See, for example, Salzberg and Thurman, cited above. Tenzin Robert Thurman is professor of Indo-Tibetan Buddhist Studies at Columbia University.

18 Carlyle, *Sartor Resartus*, 144.

19 Ibid., 149.

20 To be sure, Carlyle's reputation underwent changes throughout the twentieth century. In the 1930s and 1940s, for example, he was attacked for harboring fascist views; in the 1950s his stock rose in part because of an increasing appreciation of his prose inspired by New Criticism.

21 The list of writers Carlyle influenced includes Mill, Ruskin, Dickens, Tennyson, Browning, the Brontës, Arnold, George Eliot, Morris, and Wilde; outside England, Carlyle influenced Emerson, Whitman, Melville, Nietzsche, Proust, Gide, and Borges.

22 *English Prose of the Victorian Era*, ed. Charles Frederick Harrold and William D. Templeman (New York: Oxford University Press, 1938).

23 *Norton Anthology of English Literature*, 11th edition, ed. Stephen Greenblatt, et al. (New York: W.W. Norton, 2024). Selections from Carlyle's works appear on pp. 41–6 and 86–106.

24 To give some examples: literary critics have frequently pointed to Brontë's racist portrait of the Creole Bertha Mason in *Jane Eyre*, Mill's theory of "benevolent despotism" over colonized areas, and Dickens' defense of Governor Eyre's brutal suppression of rebellion in Jamaica in 1865.

25 *Victorian Literature 1830*–1900, ed. Dorothy Mermin and Herbert F. Tucker (Fort Worth: Harcourt College Publishers, 2002), 164. The editors of this anthology are two well-known Victorianists. In their brief introduction to Carlyle, they acknowledge *Sartor Resartus* and *The French Revolution* to be "Carlyle's masterpieces" but claim, rather defensively, that these works are "resistant to anthologization" (164). In fact, the opposite is true. *The French Revolution* contains powerful set pieces, like the taking of the Bastille, that are easily understood on their own. The chapters in *Sartor Resartus* involving Diogenes' spiritual crisis work nicely as a self-contained coming-of-age narrative, the classic *bildung* narrative of the nineteenth century that would have no small influence on Dickens' portrait of Pip's self-annihilating, self-constructing project of revaluation in *Great Expectations* and Dorothea Brooke's moral crisis in Chapter 80 of George Eliot's *Middlemarch.* It is ironic that students who use this anthology in a course encounter Smiles' *Self-Help* but miss out on the pre-eminent work on self-development of the nineteenth century.

26 Carlyle, *Sartor Resartus*, 195.

27 Friedrich Nietzsche, *Twilight of the Idols, the Portable Nietzsche*, ed. Walter Kaufman (New York: Viking, 1954), 513.

28 Collini, "Mainly Puddling," 43.

29 George Eliot, "Thomas Carlyle," *Essays of George Eliot*, ed. T. Pinney (London: Routledge, [1855] 1963), 213–14.

30 Carlyle, *Sartor Resartus*, 130.

Chapter 8

1 James Baldwin, *Notes of a Native Son* (New York: Dial Press, 1963), 87.

2 Ibid., 101–2.

3 Ibid., 102.

4 Baldwin contemplated different aspects of his past throughout his life in many non-fiction publications including *Nobody Knows My Name, The Fire Next Time, No Name in the Street*, and various essays collected in *The Price of the Ticket* and *The Cross of Redemption: Uncollected Writings.*

5 Robert Jones Jr., "The Essential James Baldwin," *New York Times* (February 28, 2024). https://www.nytimes.com/article/james-baldwin-best-books.html

6 Oorde Coombs, "The Devil Finds Work," *New York Times* (May 2, 1976). https://archive.nytimes.com/www.nytimes.com/books/98/03/29/specials/baldwin-devil.html

7 James Baldwin, *The Devil Finds Work* (New York: Vintage, 1976), 63.

8 James Baldwin, "From What's the Reason Why? A Symposium by Best-Selling Authors: James Baldwin on Another Country," *The Cross of Redemption: Uncollected Writings* (New York: Pantheon, 2010), 40.

9 Baldwin, *The Devil Finds Work,* 10.

10 Charles Dickens, *David Copperfield* (New York: W.W. Norton, 1990), 54.

11 Baldwin, *The Devil Finds Work,* 3.

12 Ibid., 4.

13 Ibid., 5. A young white school teacher named Orilla Miller took ten-year-old Baldwin in hand, directed his first play, gave him books to read, took him to movies and to a play, and visited and helped his family.

14 Ibid., 5.

15 Ibid., 6.

16 Ibid.

17 Ibid., 15.

18 Ibid., 11.

19 Ibid., 12.

20 Ibid., 29.

21 Ibid.

22 Ibid., 30.

23 Ibid., 31.

24 Ibid., 35.

25 Ibid., 33.

26 Baldwin, "The Fire Next Time," *The Price of the Ticket: Collected Nonfiction 1948–1985* (New York: St. Martin's, 1985), 348.

27 Baldwin, *The Devil Finds Work*, 34.

28 Ibid., 35.

29 Ibid., 47.

30 Ibid., 53.

31 Ibid., 60.

32 Ibid., 69.

33 Ibid., 74.

34 See Baldwin, *The Devil Finds Work*, 79. As for the doctor's sexual restraint (he does not want to consummate the relationship until the parents give their permission for the couple to marry), Baldwin writes: "No man in love is so easily prepared to surrender his beloved, or travel so many thousands of miles to do so: no one expects such behavior from Steve McQueen" (73). White fear of the sexual threat that Black men pose to white women is a theme of Part 2.

35 David Leeming, *James Baldwin* (New York: Arcade, 1994), 332–3.

36 Michael Wood, *America in the Movies* (New York: Columbia University Press, 1975), 192.

37 Ibid., 163.

38 Baldwin, *The Devil Finds Work*, 101.

39 Ibid., 121.

40 See, for example, biographies by James Campbell (*Talking at the Gates: A Life of James Baldwin* [New York: Faber, 1991]) and W.J. Weatherby, *James Baldwin: Artist on Fire, A Portrait* (New York: Dutton, 1989). For a review of these biographies, see "White Man's Heaven" by Michael Wood, who shares my view that Baldwin broke with the "articulated belief" of the church (*London Review of Books* 13, no. 3 [February 7, 1991]. https://www.lrb.co.uk/the-paper/v13/n03/michael-wood/white-man-s-heaven). Baldwin's authorized biographer, David Leeming, acknowledges Baldwin's departure from the church more fully than do Campbell and Weatherby. Bill V. Mullen's recent, politically focused biography recognizes the break with the Black church but Baldwin's subsequent embrace of a creedless religion is given little attention. (See *James Baldwin Living in Fire* [London: Pluto Press, 2019].) Baldwin's condemnation of the Christian Church in history appears in many of his works. In "An Open Letter to the Born Again," for example, he writes: "It has always astounded me that no one appears to be able to make the connection between Franco's Spain, for example, and the Spanish Inquisition; the role of the Christian Church or—to be brutally precise, the Catholic Church—in the history of Europe, and the fate of the Jews; and the role of the Jews in Christendom and the discovery of America. For the discovery of America coincided with the Inquisition, and the expulsion of the Jews from Spain. Does no one see the connection between *The Merchant of Venice* and *The Pawnbroker*? In both of these works, as though no time had passed, the Jew is portrayed as doing the Christian's usurious dirty work" (*The Price of the Ticket: Collected Nonfiction 1948–1985* [New York: St. Martin's, 1985], 655).

41 Leeming, *James Baldwin*, 28.

42 Baldwin, *The Devil Finds Work*, 12.

43 Ibid., 119.

44 Leeming, *James Baldwin*, 335.

45 James Baldwin, "To Crush a Serpent," *The Cross of Redemption: Uncollected Writings* (New York: Pantheon, 2010), 164. Baldwin writes: "I was challenged to discover for myself the meaning of the word 'transgressor.'... This challenge became the key to my journey through the Bible." Baldwin's biographer calls this essay a "final version of the Baldwin gospel, a prophet's cry for sanity" (Leeming, *James Baldwin*, 369).

46 Baldwin, *The Price of the Ticket*, 316. See also Baldwin's last important work, *Just above My Head*, in which a character says, "The song does not belong to the singer. The singer is found by the song. Ain't no singer, anywhere, ever *made up* a song—that is not possible. He *hears* something." Qtd. in Leeming, *James Baldwin*, 351.

47 Baldwin, *The Devil Finds Work*, 119.

48 Ibid., 120.

49 Leeming discusses Baldwin's statements about his religious views when he was nearing death: "He [Baldwin] did not 'believe' in God, but he felt—especially when he was alone—that there was 'something out there'" (Leeming, *James Baldwin*, 384).

50 Baldwin, *The Devil Finds Work*, 121.

51 Ibid., 122.

52 Ibid., 126.

53 Franz Kafka, *The Blue Octavo Notebooks*, ed. Max Brod, trans. Ernst Kaiser and Eithne Wilkins (Cambridge: Exact Exchange, 1991), 96.

54 Baldwin, *The Devil Finds Work*, 126–7.

55 Baldwin, *Notes of a Native Son*, 11.

56 Baldwin, Interview on *The Dick Cavett Show*, 1968. https://www.youtube.com/watch?v=WWwOi17WHpE

57 Baldwin, *Notes of a Native Son*, 11.

58 Louis Menand, "The Lives and Loves of James Baldwin," *The New Yorker* (August 18, 2025), 57–63, 58.

Chapter 9

1 Rosmarie and Keith Waldrop, *Keeping/the window open: interviews, statements, alarms, excursions/*, ed. Ben Lerner (Seattle and New York: Wave Books, 2019), 348. The statement is taken from the Preface to *A Century in Two Decades: A Burning Deck Anthology, 1961–1981*, ed. Keith Waldrop and Ben Lerner (Providence: Burning Deck, 1982).

2 In 1997 Waldrop wrote: "In *Light While There Is Light* I tried to give a sense, not of my early life, but of the world I passed through in that life. I can say of this work, as of that one: nothing here is absolutely true, and none of it entirely false." From Rosmarie and Keith Waldrop, "Ceci n'est pas Keith/Ceci n'est pas Rosmarie," *Keeping/the window open*, 42.

3 Keith Waldrop, *Light While There Is Light* (Champaign, London, Dublin: Dalkey Archive Press, [1993] 2013), 72.

4 Jaimy Gordon, "Introduction," *Light While There Is Light* (Champaign, London, Dublin: Dalkey Archive Press, 2013), xi.

5 John Updike, "Twisted Apples," *Harper's* 268, no. 1,606 (1984): 96.

6 Waldrop, *Light While There Is Light,* 201.

7 Ibid., 18–19.

8 Anton Chekhov, "To A.S. Suvorin (May 30, 1888)," "Selections from Chekhov's Letters," *Anton Chekhov's Short Stories*, ed. and trans. Ralph Matlaw (New York: Norton, 1979), 270.

9 Waldrop, *Light While There Is Light,* 16.

10 Ben Lerner, "Keith Waldrop's Haunted Realism," *The New Yorker* (February 25, 2013). https://www.newyorker.com/books/page-turner/keith-waldrops-haunted-realism

11 Waldrop, *Light While There Is Light*, 139.

12 Ibid., 197.

13 Ibid., 40.

14 Ibid., 40–3.

15 Ibid., 53.

16 Ibid., 85.

17 Ibid., 136.

18 Ibid., 155.

19 Ibid., 164–5.

20 John Keats, "Letter to George and Thomas Keats" (December 22, 1817). https://en.wikisource.org/wiki/Letter_to_George_and_Thomas_Keats,_December_28,_1817

INDEX

Page reference followed by "n" refers to end notes